International Securities Lending

International Securities Lending

Editor: **Judith Mabry**

M

© Macmillan Publishers Ltd, 1992

Reprinted 1993

All rights reserved. No part of this publication may be
reproduced or transmitted, in any form or by any means,
without permission.

Published in the United States and Canada by
STOCKTON PRESS, 1992
257 Park Avenue South, New York, N.Y. 10010, USA

ISBN 1-56159-024-X

First published in the United Kingdom by
MACMILLAN PUBLISHERS LTD, 1992
Distributed by Globe Book Services Ltd
Brunel Road, Houndmills,
Basingstoke, Hants RG21 2XS, England

ISBN 0-333-56922-3

A catalogue record for this book
is available from The British Library.

While every care has been taken in compiling the
information contained in this publication, the publishers
and editor accept no responsibility for any errors or
omissions.

Typeset and printed in Great Britain

Contents

Contributors	viii
Preface *Judith G. Mabry*	xi
Introduction: Securities Lending *Simon Luhr*	1

PART I

1 The UK Gilts and Equities Markets — 9
Patrick Mitford-Slade
History — 9
The Gilt-edged market — 10
The equity and fixed interest market — 16

2 Securities Lending in the German Market — 20
Douglas G. Ziurys and Gunter H. Femers
The long and hard road to securities lending 1986–1990: major market factors affecting rapid development — 21
Major market developments in 1990: securities lending finally established as a viable product — 26
Current status of securities lending in Germany: the Deutscher Kassenverein system — 27
The current status of securities lending in Germany: alternatives to the KV lending programme — 37
Legal and accounting aspects — 41
Required changes and future prospects for securities lending in Germany — 42

3 The French Market — 47
Michel Sidier
Structure of the securities industry — 47
The settlement system — 51
Who can lend and who can borrow: the Law of 1987 — 57
The existing lending techniques on the French market — 59

	The securities lending market	62
	Conclusion	64
4	**Lending Securities in Japan**	66
	Jiro Takahashi and Makoto Yokota	
	History of the Japan Securities Finance Co Ltd	66
	Domestic lending	67
	International lending	73
	The present situation for international lending	78
	The outlook for domestic and international lending of Japanese stocks	79
5	**Financing transactions as short-term investments**	80
	Steven R. Meier	
	Introduction to the United States market for repurchase agreements	81
	The mechanics of repos	82
	Repo collateral	83
	Types of repos	84
	Delivery of repo collateral	84
	Determination of repo and reverse repo rates	86
	The matched book	87
	Dealer's availability of repo collateral	88
	Parties involved in the repo market	90
	Repurchase agreements: a hybrid transaction	90
	The evolution of the repo market	91
	Financing transactions and the 'Big Picture'	96
	International financing transactions	97
	XYZ Bank – February 1990	99
	Suggested guidelines for investing in 'repurchase agreements'	102
	Summary	102

PART II

1	**Risks in International Securities Lending – Identification and Minimisation**	107
	Habib Motani	
	Essential elements of a securities loan	107
	Main areas of risk	108
	Credit risk	109
	Default	112
	Operational risks	113
	Conclusion	115

2 Global Custody — 116
Daniel R. Roccato

Functions of a global custodian — 117
Evolution of global custody — 120
Image — 122

3 The Function of the Clearing House — 124
Securities Lending in an International Clearing System: Cedel's Securities Lending Programme
Susan Alexander

4 The Euroclear System — 132
Martine Dinne

5 The Taxation of International Lending Transactions — 140
Jurgen Jung

Introduction — 140
Tax treatment of securities lending transactions in Germany — 141
Tax treatment of securities lending transactions in France — 144
Tax treatment of securities lending transactions in Japan — 149
Accounting and tax treatment of securities lending transactions in the UK — 150
Tax treatment of securities lending transactions in the United States — 152

Index — 155

Contributors

Susan Alexander joined Cedel, Luxembourg, in 1989. Since then she has had a range of responsibilities which have included being project manager for securities lending, overseeing customer documentation, and developing computer based training. Before Cedel, Susan was a vice-president at Oppenheimer & Co., New York, working first as director of commodities research and later in fixed income product development and international securities trading. Previously, she worked at Kidder, Peabody in their futures department.

Martine Dinne, Managing Director, heads the Euroclear Strategic Research and Product Management Group. The group conducts research on markets and Participant service requirements which defines service upgrades and new market and instrument priorities. She joined the Euroclear Operations Centre in 1969 and became Area Manager in 1984, after serving as Account Manager for Belgian, French and UK accounts. In 1985 she was promoted to assume responsibility of the newly-created Strategic Research Group.

Günter H. Femers is a Vice-President and Manager of the Securities Liquidity Management group at J. P. Morgan GmbH in Frankfurt. His previous assignment was marketing various operational services to international brokers/dealers and banks. Prior to joining J. P. Morgan in 1985, he worked on project and export finance with Commerzbank.

Jürgen Jung is a tax partner in the Frankfurt office of Arthur Andersen & Co., and specialises in the areas of capital markets and the financial services industry. From the outset of the firm's activities to establish the German Exchange for Options and Financial Futures, he was responsible for the non-systems area during a three-year assignment. He has published several articles on the tax and accounting treatment of financial instruments and speaks at seminars on this topic.

Simon Luhr is a Senior Vice-President at Nomura Securities International, New York. A widely known expert in the domestic and international securities lending business, he was previously at Morgan Stanley in London where he had worked since 1986, most recently as worldwide head of the firm's international securities lending. Prior to that, he worked for James Capel and Citicorp Scrimgeour Vickers in London.

Judith G. Mabry is a Vice-President with Morgan Stanley & Co., New York. She has been with Morgan Stanley since 1981 in a variety of roles involving securities lending and repo. These include US Marketing Manager for domestic/international securities lending with MS Securities Services Inc, product development for international securities lending with Morgan Stanley Global Securities Services and Product Manager for International Securities lending with Morgan Stanley Fixed Income Division. She has spent time working in both the Tokyo and London offices of Morgan Stanley, and is now based in New York. Prior to joining Morgan Stanley she spent four years at Salomon Brothers.

Steven R. Meier is currently a Vice-President and Trading Manager with Merrill Lynch, New York, and is responsible for their worldwide non-dollar financing activities. In addition, he is the Product Manager for all automated repo programs, bond borrowing and securities lending activities. Upon graduation he joined Merrill Lynch's Capital Markets Training Program and is a member of the Finance Trading department. He possesses an extensive background in financing and matched book trading activities involving US treasuries and agencies, money market instruments, various mortgage-backed securities and a full range of international debt obligations.

Patrick Mitford-Slade is a partner in Cazenove & Co. and Managing Director of Cazenove Money Brokers. He was a member of the Stock Exchange Council between 1976 and 1991, Deputy Chairman of the Exchange from 1982 to 1985, and is still a member of the Gilt Edged Market Committee. He has been closely involved with the Exchange's market and technical developments, including the Central Gilts Office project, for several years. He was Chairman of the Securities Industry Steering Committee on TAURUS (SISCOT) and is now Chairman of the TAURUS Rules Committee. He has been in charge of Cazenove's stock lending activities since 1972 and is Chairman of the Money Brokers Association.

Habib Motani is a solicitor and a partner of Clifford Chance. He is a member of Clifford Chance's International Financial Markets Practice and Head of its Derivative Products Group. He has been with Clifford Chance for some 14 years and during that period has undertaken considerable work in relation to derivative products (including risk assessment) and other money market and capital markets instruments, netting and payment and settlement systems as well as a wide range of financing transactions.

Daniel R. Roccato began his career in the financial services industry with Morgan Stanley International, London, in 1986. Prior to joining Morgan Stanley he taught economics for two years in the USA. In 1987 he was assigned to Morgan Stanley & Co., New York, where he was a start-up member of a project team which managed the firm's entry into the global custody business. He has also worked with the network management team with regional responsibility for Europe and subsequently the Far East. In 1990 he returned to London and is currently Vice-President with overall responsibility for Morgan Stanley Global Securities Services (MSGS) in the UK.

Michel Sidier was born in Paris and educated at H.E.C. in Paris followed by an MBA at Columbia University, New York. In 1972 he joined Banque Indosuez, Paris, where he occupied various positions before moving to Australia and South Africa on behalf of the bank. In 1987 he was transferred to London to head the new International Securities Lending desk. He returned to Paris in 1992 to take up a new position with J. P. Morgan.

Jiro Takahashi is an Associate Director, Head of Systems and Head of Treasury of Mitsubishi Bank, London. He has been with Mitsubishi Bank since 1975 after graduating from Keio University. Since then he has worked in Tokyo and Osaka before joining the London office in January 1990.

Makoto Yokota joined the Sumitimo Trust and Banking Co Ltd in 1984 where his responsibilities have included being Officer for Private Banking, Assistant Manager for Custody Services and, more recently, Manager for Securities Lending and Custody Services.

Douglas G. Ziurys is a Vice-President and Manager of the Securities Trust & Information Services group at J. P. Morgan GmbH, Frankfurt. His responsibilities include the marketing of DEM securities lending, clearing, custody, and execution services. Prior to joining J. P. Morgan in 1986, he managed a representative office in Hamburg for CoreStates Financial Corp. Before entering banking, he worked in the electronics industry as a product line marketing manager.

Preface

International securities lending has become an increasingly important market over the last six or seven years. This product is growing and expanding into new countries as tax, legal and regulatory barriers are being toppled. More and more countries are accepting the importance and necessity of securities lending. Opportunities continue to grow for participants in the securities lending market. With the endorsement of the Group of Thirty, added credibility and support has been given to this product.

This book is intended to serve as a comprehensive guide to the origins, development, current status, and future direction of the international securities lending market. In a series of chapters written by industry professionals – bankers, brokers, lawyers and tax experts – both broad overviews and specific issues are presented. The contributions of each author reflect their personal experiences and opinions, making this a timely and inside view of a rapidly-evolving product.

Chapters cover the five major marketplaces in which securities lending has taken hold: Germany is profiled by Douglas Ziurys and Günter Femers; France by Michel Sidier; the USA by Steven R. Meier; Japan by Jiro Takahashi and Makoto Yokota; and the UK by Patrick Mitford-Slade. Countries not covered were not omitted due to lack of interest or importance, but due to time, energy and space constraints.

An assessment of the risks involved in securities lending is skilfully addressed by Habib Motani of Clifford Chance. His chapter outlines the major issues on which every participant in this market should focus. Jürgen Jung of Arthur Andersen ably tackles the somewhat daunting task of presenting the major tax issues for each of the five countries covered.

The major role which the Global Custodian plays in this market, as well as the importance of the two major clearing houses, Euroclear and Cedel, is also discussed. Understanding how these institutions operate is key to appreciating the basic building blocks of securities lending.

Several of our contributors, particularly Michel Sidier and Patrick Mitford-Slade, have given a very thorough overview of the structure and operation of their local markets. This was intended to help the reader appreciate where and how securities lending fits into the day-to-day trading and settlement of securities. In many cases it is critical to understand the cash and derivative markets in order to appreciate the significant role of securities lending. Our contributors have attempted to provide this insight.

With constantly changing markets, timeliness is key to understanding securities lending. We have attempted to compile material in this book that is both broad and detailed, while remaining up to date. Every effort has been made by the contributors to keep the information as current as possible up to the time the manuscript goes to press. Many revisions and rewrites have made this possible. My thanks go to the contributors for their patience and perseverance in this effort.

Please use this book as a guide to the basics of international securities lending. As always, consult with your own tax and legal advisers before entering into any new product.

Thanks also to the financial editors at Macmillan Press for giving us the opportunity to put together this volume on International Securities Lending. A tremendous amount of information and knowledge has been compressed into a relatively small volume by the hard work of the contributors, with the guidance of Macmillan Press. They have made my task as Editor much simpler than originally imagined!

Judith G. Mabry
New York
May, 1992

Introduction: Securities Lending
Simon Luhr

Securities lending is growing fast. Its rapid expansion in recent years looks set to continue as this exciting process proves its value by producing generous profits.

The beauty of securities lending is that everyone benefits from it. Institutions gather extra income from securities that would otherwise be collecting dust in a depository. Broker dealers enhance their flexibility to trade. The market benefits from increased liquidity in which broker dealers can trade freely, knowing that they will not be trapped in unwanted positions because the market has slowed up.

Securities lending began in London's coffee shops in the late nineteenth century with the borrowing of gilt edged stocks. A broker with a short-term delivery problem would borrow shares from an associate to cover him while he awaited the arrival of the correct stock. In a largely unregulated and informal market where a man's word was his bond, securities lending was a process by which the market could be kept going while the paperwork caught up with its movements.

As the market grew, so did its bureaucracy. By early this century the practice had become more common and securities were being loaned in a more structured market-place. In the mid-1960s securities lending expanded into equities. It covered traders against the vagaries of the postal system, and of the slow, manual task of transferring the ownership of securities which involved the movement of certificates and transfer forms going back and forth between companies specialising in registration. Long settlement cycles are the bane of a trader's working life, and in an active market it made sense to borrow securities to fulfil a commitment. When the original securities arrived, the loan was returned with a fee for the lender's trouble.

Demand increased, and some firms began to specialise in borrowing and lending various forms of securities for settlement and trading reasons. A few went a step further and opened up separate capitalised companies dealing only with securities lending – evidence of a healthy market with good growth prospects.

For many years securities lending inhabited only domestic market-places. The practice soon followed the brokers and institutional investors as they started to focus more globally in the late 1970s and early 1980s. The leaders in the trend were UK and US broker dealers who began to apply local trading techniques to their international operations. As foreign brokers joined, the Tokyo Stock Exchange applied new trading techniques and the demand to borrow overseas securities grew.

By this time the securities lending market itself had become far more sophisticated. Companies had become more adventurous in raising funds and began to issue various kinds of securities, many of them convertible back into the underlying equity at a later stage. As derivative products, such as traded options and convertible bonds, started to develop, so did opportunities to trade them against one another. To limit a trading risk brokers would hedge by selling one security, and holding on to the other. This also became a trading technique when price disparities emerged between the two products.

In these trading strategies, brokers were selling securities that they owned in a different form, and were unable to deliver against the underlying sale commitment. In some cases the broker would fulfil his delivery requirement by requesting to convert the derivative into the underlying shares – which could still leave the problem of the difference in settlement dates. Pressures of high financing costs and exposure to the market-place created situations in which brokers needed the option of borrowing securities for a short period to fulfil a commitment.

The success of this technique led some brokers to feel comfortable taking longer positions where they would hedge one product versus another for longer periods. They were helped in this by the improved research and information services which gave them an incentive to pursue both long- and short-term strategies. Trading strategies which involve hedging are a major source of growth in today's market.

As brokers demands grew and the business became more specialised, firms set up special units responsible for supplying securities to fulfil settlement and trading needs. However, most institutional investors were still reluctant to lend their securities. They were concerned with the lack of regulation in the market and with the perceived risk, and indeed with the very concept of lending an asset to a third party. The emergence of regulations to control and monitor all aspects of trading, including securities lending, helped give securities holders more confidence in the idea.

However, some reluctance has remained. The much-improved standard of communication between brokers, lenders and regulators should allow everyone to feel comfortable with the idea while leaving a framework in which the market is able to develop.

Traditional roles in securities lending are changing. Once, securities borrowers fell into one of two categories: they were either a broker dealer borrowing for his own need, or a separate capitalised company borrowing to reloan. Today, the specialised firms remain, but the broker dealers have gained such a supply of securities to lend that their own demand is not great enough to fulfil the institutional lenders' revenue expectations. Consequently, most broker dealers also lend to fellow broker dealers to meet their trading and settlement requirements.

The institutional investor has several reasons to lend. Securities are usually bought for investment and income, though there can be strategic reasons too. By lending them out, the fund manager generates extra income through the fee, increasing the yield on the portfolio of stocks he holds. He may, on the other hand, lend to offset his trading and holding costs. Cross-border investment can be an expensive business because of the custodians' fees for holding securities in their depots, as well as the cost of moving stock in and out. Lending securities helps to pay these charges.

Lenders may fear that a broker dealer they deal with will run into financial difficulty and be unable to return the borrowed securities, losing the full value of these assets. Protection is provided through the institution receiving some form of collateral. He could liquidate this and buy back the securities in the market to replace the lost assets. Thus it is crucial for the lender to deal with a broker who provides sufficient collateral to cover any default.

Broker dealers have two reasons to borrow securities: fails and trading strategy. In both cases, he would borrow the securities to optimise the profitability of the trade, and to limit the counterparty risks. Fails can be very costly as he incurs more operational costs in solving the problem and effecting delivery of the securities. Also, if he is unable to make delivery, he will not be paid. Finally, like the lender, he is exposed to the counterparty he has sold the securities to. If they run into trouble, he could be left holding a position he no longer requires. Borrowing securities avoids all three problems, which is why the practice has grown so fast in recent years.

Borrowing to cover a trading strategy can take a number of forms. A broker might sell a security early, believing he will be able to buy it back later at a lower price, thereby making a profit. Or he might take advantage of price differences between a derivative and an underlying equity by going long one instrument and short another. His position would then be unwound by either converting one security into the other, or by unwinding the position by buying back the short position and selling out the long one.

In some countries failing to settle can result in suspension, therefore, it is essential for the broker to borrow the securities in order to meet his obligation, and avoid a penalty from the local exchange. Borrowing may also be necessary when settlement dates differ between local brokers, local participants, and foreign institutions trading the same security. So a broker selling a security on the local exchange may have to settle in two business days, while the securities seller may have a more generous deadline – requiring the broker to borrow the securities for the intervening period.

By borrowing the securities, the broker dealer effects delivery and gathers payment from the purchaser. He can use this money to pay the lender, who can in turn use it as collateral against the borrow.

Intermediaries play a vital role in the smooth working of any security borrowing and lending arrangement. Their responsibility is to find a supply of securities available to be lent. This is achieved by marketing the product to institutional investors.

Potential lenders invariably require a great deal of information before getting involved in securities lending. They must be confident that their assets will be protected and that they will not be exposed to market risk. When he agrees to lend, he may do the work himself or sub-contract it out to a custodian. The intermediary is there to advise the lender on how to maximise his return, and to point out any possible pitfalls, especially in international deals. Clearly the lender must be assured that even though he is no longer the registered owner of the securities, he will continue to receive income from them.

Intermediaries are often principals in lending transactions, therefore it is paramount that they offer financial stability, for they provide the lender with collateral and pay the fees due on the outstanding loan contract. They also advise on tax and regulatory issues existing in the countries the lender wishes to deal in. The basic concept of borrowing and lending – the simultaneous transfer of securities from an institutional investor to a broker dealer in return for collateral of at least the value of the securities – may sound very simple. But once you are dealing in international equity securities around the globe the practice is complicated by variations in settlement procedure and time zone differences. Securities are settled in different ways in different market-places around the world, sometimes incurring unforeseen costs such as stamp duty or re-registration charges.

Once a lender has agreed to become involved, the intermediary brings the new supply to the market-place to allow broker dealers to borrow it. It is therefore important that the intermediary understands why broker dealers are borrowing the securities, and what the future market trends are, so that he can ensure the supply is available when required.

Acting as principal in both sides of the transaction, the intermediary must ensure that he receives collateral from the borrower and pledges collateral to the lender in appropriate amounts on the right day. He also pays and collects fees charged on the business, ensures the smooth settlement of the securities, and the paying and collecting of any dividend or corporate action. Carrying out these important tasks is expensive in terms of systems and technology, as well as in terms of people with local market expertise. A global presence is required to communicate with broker dealers, who often trade in more than one country, and with lenders who may be based in yet another country, possibly in a different time zone.

An intermediary needs to be able to operate within the different settlement requirements that apply around the world, ensuring smooth settlements around the globe, often with different counterparties. The last thing a broker dealer wants is to borrow securities to cover a fail and then find he has fails on the trade and on the stock borrowed to clean up the original fail.

A good intermediary will provide a 24-hour service to broker dealers, and maximise lenders' revenue opportunities by being able to lend from his portfolio in time zones and regions outside his usual reach. Broker dealers who already have a global presence in a number of markets are particularly well equipped to set up an intermediary function which can call on this network.

Collateral is the primary tool for reducing counterparty exposure, thus reducing any risks in a deal. The form it takes is agreed between the two principal parties and is usually cash, government bonds, treasury bills, certificates of deposit, or letters of credit. It is generally accepted that the securities lender will require a margin of between 2 and 5 per cent above the market value of the securities loaned. This covers any extra exposure that may be incurred with the day-to-day fluctuation of the underlying security on the foreign exchange market, and any costs and brokerage fees of buying in the securities in the event of a default.

As the price of the securities on loan changes, so will the margin on the collateral. It is therefore accepted practice that the parties carry out a mark-to-market function. This means that all securities on loan are re-priced each day to arrive at a new market value. If the value rises the lender will require a pledge of extra collateral, and if the value falls the broker dealer will require repayment of collateral to bring it in line with the new margin. Following this procedure on a daily basis assures both counterparties that collateral is in place, minimising their risk in the transaction.

In theory, stock lending involves the simultaneous transfer of collateral and securities, but this is not always possible. For example, if a US broker dealer borrows Japanese securities in Tokyo and pays cash collateral in US dollars, the different time zones and different currencies may mean that the securities and collateral move separately. This is known as daylight exposure. It is important to limit exposure on security lending as much as possible, and the key is to know your counterpart.

A lender should feel most comfortable lending to a highly capitalised intermediary owned by a parent which is also well capitalised. Most of the regulators who govern this business have taken the level of collateral and the daylight exposure as the principal method of measuring risk and exposure. An intermediary without the correct level of collateral in place, or who has not monitored exposure accurately, would have to use their own capital as the penalty for this mismanagement. Further reassurance is provided by the regulators of equity stock lending who generally require a loan agreement to be in place between all counterparties which highlights the rights of each party to the procedure in the event that one party defaults.

Some tax and regulatory barriers which hinder market liquidity are being removed, increasing the potential for expansion of the international security lending market. Furthermore, various new products in the futures and options trading fields now require the borrowing of securities. There is potential for growth as more clients start to focus on new forms of global investing, and as it becomes more necessary, and far easier, to borrow and lend securities. As markets become more efficient, and as settlement becomes cheaper, borrowing costs for broker dealers will be reduced, as will lenders' participant costs. This will make it more economic for both parties to be actively involved in this dynamic market-place.

Part I

1: The UK Gilts and Equities Markets

Patrick Mitford-Slade, Cazenove, London

In contrast to the procedures described in some other chapters of this publication, stock lending in UK domestic securities still takes place in a relatively closely regulated environment. The main reason for this is the peculiarity to the UK of the competing market maker system for dealing in securities.

In both the government bond (gilt-edged) and UK equity and bond markets, only those firms who are providing liquidity to the system by taking on the obligation of making a continuous two-way market have the privilege of being able to borrow securities to settle their transactions. Brokers may not borrow securities for settling their own or their clients' bargains since this might enable them to compete with the market makers as 'fair weather' traders.

Borrowing may only take place in order to enable a market maker to fulfil a contract to sell securities (or to replace an existing loan which has been called by a lender). Stock may not be borrowed for any other purpose, such as denying its availability to a rival.

All borrowing and lending of domestic securities has historically taken place through regulated intermediaries known as money brokers but, with the increasing internationalisation of securities markets, it is possible that this may change – at least in the equity market – in the foreseeable future.

HISTORY

Stock lending in gilt-edged securities originated in the second half of the nineteenth century when several specialist firms were involved in financing that market. They became known as 'money brokers'. The money broking system matured with the rapid growth of the gilt-edged market during the twentieth century.

The lending of UK equities and loan stocks began in the 1960s and reached its peak in mid-1987. The high volumes of turnover by the growing number of market makers after Big Bang led to a 'paper crunch' and a large settlement backlog. Levels of stock lending retreated after the Bank of England stepped in to demand that market makers should put up increased margin on their stock loans, and was reduced further after the market crash of October that year. The level now fluctuates with the level of activity in the market and, particularly, with opportunities that may arise for market makers to arbitrage between futures, options and the underlying stocks.

The lending of overseas stocks to UK market makers started in the early 1970s and has grown with the increasing internationalisation of London. Lending of international securities does not have to take place through Stock Exchange money brokers and therefore forms a relatively small but growing part of their overall book. The description of this market is covered elsewhere in this volume.

THE GILT-EDGED MARKET

Market Structures

At the time of writing, there were 18 registered market makers in gilt-edged securities who have undertaken to the Bank of England to make a continuous market in a full range of gilt-edged securities. The Bank is the regulator of the gilt-edged market and has granted the market makers the privilege of borrowing stock in return for taking on this obligation. The Bank is anxious that stock borrowing should be strictly controlled and has laid down that it may only take place through Stock Exchange money brokers who are themselves regulated by the Bank. There are currently eight firms of Stock Exchange money brokers (see Figure 1), of whom three originated in the last century, one joined the market in 1972 and the remainder in 1986/87. Two others, who joined the market in 1972, have recently closed down.

Lenders of gilt-edged securities have to be approved as such by the Bank of England and the Inland Revenue. Authorised lenders include banks, insurance companies, pension funds, building societies, investment trusts and companies. Individual investors are not so authorised.

Supervision

The central participants in the gilt-edged market fall under the direct supervision of the Bank's Gilt-Edged Division. Market makers, inter-dealer brokers and Stock Exchange money brokers are all required to establish separately capitalised companies, and their permitted levels of business are calculated on a risk weighting basis related to the company's capital base. The different weights allocated to various aspects of the business reflect the

Stock Exchange Money Brokers

Money Broker	Parent Company
Cazenove Money Brokers	Cazenove & Co.
King & Shaxson Money Brokers Ltd.	King & Shaxson Holdings Plc
LM (Moneybrokers) Ltd.	Gerrard & National Holdings Plc
Lazard Money Broking Ltd.	Lazard Brothers & Co. Ltd.
Lehman Brothers Money Brokers Ltd.	Shearson Lehman Brothers Holdings Plc
Prudential Bache Capital Funding (Money Brokers) Ltd.	The Prudential Insurance Company of America
Rowe & Pitman Moneybroking Ltd.	S.G. Warburg Group Plc
Sheppards Moneybrokers Ltd.	Catel-Allen Holdings Plc

Figure 1.1

Gilt Edged Stock Lending Volumes January – September 1991

Date	Amount Outstanding
7.1.91	5,332
4.2.91	5,209
4.3.91	5,366
8.4.91	4,889
7.5.91	5,416
10.6.91	5,414
8.7.91	5,191
5.8.91	4,576
9.9.91	4,599

Source: Bank of England. December 1991

Table 1.1

Bank's view as to the credit risks involved. (The system is fully described in the paper 'The Future Structure of the Gilt Edged Market' issued by the Bank in April 1985, although the weightings have in some instances been changed since that time.)

Details of turnover and risk-weighting calculations are reported on line to the Bank daily and, in addition, there are weekly, monthly, quarterly and annual reporting requirements and quarterly interviews to enable the Bank to keep a close eye on market developments and the levels of risk.

Settlement

In accordance with the Rules of the London Stock Exchange, the settlement of gilt-edged bargains normally takes place on the business day following the transaction. In practice, delays may occur when, for example, a seller fails to deliver stock on time. In addition, market makers may sell stock which they have not yet purchased. Prompt settlement of sales can, of course, be made by the borrowing of stock and the settlement of purchases by the borrowing of money. Market makers are therefore able to make a market in substantial sized bargains to meet the needs of the institutional market, and are able to run substantial bear or bull positions to take advantage of their view of future market movements or of arbitrage opportunities. A market maker whose overall book is balanced may run a large bear position in one stock – covered by stock borrowing – against a bull position in another stock, financed by the proceeds of the bear sale.

If the market maker is a net bull or net bear, he will respectively be a net borrower or lender of money. The lending of stock and money goes hand in hand, and the Stock Exchange money broker provides the market maker with an overall stock and money management service.

Major institutional stock holdings are maintained in the Central Gilts Office (CGO) book entry transfer system which is run jointly by the Bank of England and the Stock Exchange through a Joint Management Committee. The settlement of transactions between the major participants in the market is also provided by the CGO. Each market participant will be a member of the system or, at least, have his stock held in the system and will nominate a settlement bank (one of the banks in the town clearing and CHAPS system) to act on its behalf in making and receiving payment through the CGO system.

Assured Payments

The movement of stock is carried out through computer terminals, with every movement being made against a simultaneous instruction for the payment of money. This is known as an 'assured payment'.

The assured payments system incorporates a three-way contractual relationship between the CGO, the CGO member and his settlement bank resting on two fundamental principles:

(a) The settlement bank undertakes that, at the moment the CGO transfers stock from the account of the deliverer (seller or lender) to that of the acceptor (buyer or borrower), the acceptor's bank takes on an irrevocable commitment to effect payment on the same day to the deliverer's settlement bank; and

(b) the CGO system ensures that stock can only move out of a CGO account against such an irrevocable commitment.

At all times, therefore, the settlement bank knows that it is protected either by stock on the customer's CGO account or by an irrevocable payment instruction from another settlement bank. The lender of stock is, therefore, covered by the money broker's settlement bank's commitment to make an assured payment to the lender's settlement bank, and the money broker is similarly protected by the market maker's settlement bank.

Stock Loans

Stock loans may be of almost any size from a few thousand pounds to tens of millions. They may be loans 'at call' – which, in effect, will be returned when the market maker no longer needs them – or for a fixed period. In recent years the amount of stock borrowed for fixed periods has increased dramatically as market makers arbitrage between gilts, futures, options and cash deposits. Stock is frequently borrowed fixed to redemption, particularly where the coupon (and redemption yield) on the stock is less than the rate achievable on other instruments. The overall volume of stock on loan varies little. Figures are published by the Bank three months in arrears (see Table 1).

The rate paid for the stock loan will vary depending on the type of stock and the period of the loan and is highly competitive. Typically a stock at call may cost a market maker $7/16$ per cent to $1/2$ per cent on a per annum basis, while fixed loans to redemption have been arranged at rates from $1/4$ per cent to over 1 per cent. The money broker will normally take from $1/16$ per cent to $1/8$ per cent, with the balance going to the lender. The CGO system and handling costs will absorb a substantial part of any 'turn' unless the loan is large and out for a reasonable period.

Money Loans

The lending of stock by a money broker to a market maker is secured, in the first instance, by the payment of the value of the stock (without margin) to the money broker. This is done through the assured payments system in which stock is valued at the CGO reference price established by the Bank of England at the close of business on the previous day. The market maker then has the right to borrow back this money to help fund his bull positions and will provide these stocks, or other collateral (valued to include a margin of, normally, 2½ per cent) as security for the loan. The money broker will pay the market maker a relatively low rate of interest on the original money put up as security for the stock loan, and will lend back at a small premium – being the cost of borrowing referred to above. Hence these money loans are known as 'cheap money'.

A money broker will also do his best to fulfil a market maker's request for additional money over and above the market maker's right to cheap money. Money will be generated by other market makers' bear positions and from the lending of equity and overseas stocks. Additional funds will be borrowed from banks, discount houses and, sometimes, from the Bank of England, with whom a Stock Exchange money broker has a 'last resort' borrowing facility similar to that available to the discount market and gilt-edged market makers. This money will be lent to market makers at the market rate and hence, in contrast to cheap money, is known as 'dear money'.

If a market maker does not wish to take his money back as cheap money – because he is running an overall bear book – he may leave the money with the money broker as 'money over' for which the money broker will pay an additional rate to equal, overall, the market rate less the cost of borrowing. In addition the money broker may bid for fixed-term loans from the market maker, particularly where the market maker is borrowing stock fixed to redemption.

In order to manage loans from banks and market makers, and other money generated from equity stock lending, a money broker will lend money to banks and to discount houses against collateral, or may itself run a money book of Treasury and Eligible Bills and Certificates of Deposit, which will be added to his pool of collateral.

Collateral

Apart from the use of his own capital, every loan of money by a money broker will be against collateral provided by the market maker or bank, because all stock and money loans to the money broker by a bank or institution have to be secured. Collateral in the gilt-edged market is likely to consist of one of the following forms:

(a) British Government stock
(b) Corporation and Commonwealth stock
(c) UK Government Treasury Bills
(d) Eligible Bank Bills
(e) Sterling Certificates of Deposit
(f) Local Authority bonds
(g) Bulldog bonds
(h) Letters of credit

A combination of these may be used depending on the lender's requirements.

The movement of collateral within the CGO system takes place between 2 p.m. and 3 p.m. For collateral purposes, a consideration value is specified and the system will select and transfer securities up to this value plus the agreed margin on a preset formula using first the earliest maturing security and then the next maturing and so on. This is known as 'delivery-by-value'. Collateral delivered in this form is returned automatically the following morning against an assured payment instruction. CGO collateral moved by member-to-member delivery and other types of collateral may remain in the lender's hands for a longer period than overnight.

Sterling Bonds

Bulldog bonds, which are defined as sterling fixed interest securities issued by overseas governments and institutions, may also be borrowed and lent in much the same way as gilt-edged securities. Most such bonds are held in the CGO system and dealings in these take place for next day settlement through the book entry transfer system.

Discussions are taking place between the market, the Bank of England and the Stock Exchange about the possibility of enhancing the CGO system – or the CMO (Central Moneymarkets Office) system through which money market instruments can be transferred by book-entry transfer. The objective is to handle other sterling bonds, issued for example by companies, and perhaps ECU, Eurodollar and other foreign bonds. There is a need for such instruments to be settled for next day delivery in a 'cash against delivery' book-entry system, and part of the debate is as to whether this should take place through the CGO, CMO or the imminent TAURUS system.

THE EQUITY AND FIXED INTEREST MARKET

Market Structure

The market structure for the equity market is similar to that for the gilt-edged market in that there are a number of market makers committed to making a continuous two-way price in securities who are allowed the privilege of borrowing stock. At the time of writing, there were 24 market makers active in UK equities and a further 11 in fixed interest securities including convertibles and preference shares. Some of these make markets in a wide number of securities, while others select a smaller number of securities or markets in which they specialise.

Traded option market makers may also borrow the underlying securities in which they are trading the option. It is likely that market makers in index options, in convertibles and in other derivatives will also be allowed to borrow the underlying equity securities shortly. The merged LIFFE and LTOM derivatives exchange has obtained approval from the authorities for all principal trades to be able to borrow stock and thus raises the question as to whether stock borrowing privileges will be further extended in future. This, together with other developments in the international market, creates a threat to the Stock Exchange market making structure.

As in the gilt-edged market, securities may only be borrowed through authorised intermediaries who may, in this market, be either Stock Exchange money brokers or equity only money brokers.

Lenders need to be recognised as such by the Inland Revenue and will, again, be the major institutional investors.

Supervision

There is no central regulator of equity stock lending, but the Stock Exchange is aware, through its settlement system, of the volumes of lending. On occasion the Bank of England may step in (as in 1987) if it sees a potential risk to the market in the volumes of unsettled business. The Stock Exchange money brokers handle the majority of the UK stock lending business so that the Bank keeps a close eye on the market through its regular monitoring. Equity only money brokers are regulated by and report to the Securities and Futures Authority and need not be members of the London Stock Exchange; most only carry out international stock lending business and only need to be members of the Stock Exchange (because of the Talisman settlement system) if they wish to borrow and lend UK equities.

Settlement

Stock will be borrowed by the market makers to meet their settlement obligations on account day or any other day if not dealing for account settlement. Borrowed stock is credited to the SEPON nominee in Talisman and transferred to the market maker's account on settlement day – and hence to the buyer. On settlement day the market maker pays the money broker, through the Stock Exchange's net settlement system, the value of the loan plus 5 per cent margin.

Stock may be borrowed for indefinite or fixed periods and the rate paid will depend on the terms of the loan. The overall volume of equity and fixed interest stock on loan is not published but is known to fluctuate between £1.25 billion to £2.5 billion depending on market activity.

Money Loans and Collateral

As in the gilt market, the money initially provided by market makers as collateral may be borrowed back as 'cheap money'. 'Dear money' may also be available depending upon the ease with which the money broker can place with lenders the collateral provided. Money market collateral is easily placed but equity market makers will normally wish to provide their bull positions in equity and fixed interests stocks as collateral. This is normally in the form of Talisman short-term collateral certificates which are issued by the Stock Exchange. These are overnight certificates guaranteeing to the holder (the lender) that equity stock to cover the value of the loan is being held in SEPON on his behalf.

Stock held in depositories such as Euroclear may also be acceptable to lenders as collateral.

Collateral will cover the value of the loan plus margin of, normally, 5 per cent in the case of gilt or money market collateral and 10 per cent in the case of equity (Talisman) collateral. Marking to market of loans and collateral is carried out daily, based on the previous day's Daily Official List prices.

Lenders' Rights

A lender is entitled to all dividends and other rights on stock while on loan and the majority of these will be accounted for automatically by the Talisman system. Any option on which a decision by the lender is required, such as a rights issue or a takeover, will be managed by the money broker with the borrowing market maker provided that the lender has given adequate notice. Normally, however, stock will not be lent during a takeover and will, if on loan, be recalled by the lender in time for him to accept the offer himself.

The only 'right' which cannot be organised is the right to vote; a lender wishing to exercise his vote must recall the stock in time for it to be again registered in his name. There is no guarantee, however, that stock can be returned in time for a vote or for a takeover – but the agreed procedures protect the lender in the latter case.

A lender may sell a stock on loan at any time and call for its redelivery. If it cannot be returned in time for settlement the money broker will pay the proceeds of sale to the lender and stop the rate of interest to the market maker. 'Buying-in' is not a major feature of the UK market, although it may be organised centrally by the Stock Exchange if transactions remain unsettled for over four weeks.

Legal Agreements

In December 1990, new agreements were introduced between all parties to set out the mechanics of the loan and the legal obligations in all circumstances. These agreements clarify that full right, title and interest passes in collateral as well as in the stock being lent. 'Equivalent collateral' and 'equivalent stock' is transferred back at the end of a loan. The agreements also confirm the right of 'set-off' in the event of default.

Taxation

Stock lending and the movement of collateral should have no adverse taxation consequences. No stamp duty is payable on the transfer or return of the stock; stamp duty is, in any case, due to be lifted on the introduction of TAURUS. Provided a lender has been approved, and the lending is in accordance with the legislation (ICTA, 1988 and subsequent amendments), the lending and return of securities will not be treated, for capital gains and corporation tax purposes, as a disposal or acquisition.

Income derived from stock lending is subject to income or corporation tax for all lenders, although costs incurred exclusively in stock lending may be offset against such income. Pension funds are not exempt from tax on the income derived from stock lending, because such income is not deemed to be derived from 'investments held for the purposes of the scheme'. However, the Inland Revenue has given its assurance that this will have no bearing on the tax exempt status of a pension fund's investment income, since stock lending is an integral part of a fund's investment operations and is not regarded as trading.

TAURUS and the Future

The TAURUS book-entry transfer system is being introduced in 1993. This will bring greater efficiency in settlement and will reduce the volume of stock borrowed. Rolling settlement, to follow within a few months of the introduction of TAURUS, is likely to increase the demand again, but it is likely that many loans will be for very short periods, possibly just overnight.

A delivery versus payment system will accompany rolling settlement and will allow for facilities similar to the assured payments and delivery-by-value facilities of the CGO. It may then be possible to eliminate any remaining daylight exposure from the stock lending system.

TAURUS in its early phases is only designed to allow for stock borrowing through money brokers, but more flexibility will be built into future enhancements.

Once TAURUS is fully effective, pressure for a direct stock lending system will inevitably increase. On the assumption that the competing market making system continues, it is likely that only committed market makers will be allowed by the market regulators to borrow stock, but the requirement for borrowing to be done through money brokers may be lifted. It is likely, however, that the overall service provided by money brokers in gilts, equities and money will continue to be appreciated by market makers whilst the close regulation and supervision of the money brokers will continue to give confidence to lenders.

2: Securities Lending in the German Market

Douglas G. Ziurys and Günter H. Femers,
J. P. Morgan GmbH, Frankfurt

Securities lending in the German market has been developing slowly due to various market and regulatory constraints. Significant market changes in 1990 and 1991 have altered the securities lending landscape in Germany, making it an acceptable transaction form as in more progressive markets. In this chapter, the authors trace the development of securities lending in Germany prior to the 'breakthrough' years, analyse the current situation and discuss the adjustments necessary to make securities lending a fully developed financial vehicle in the German market in the future.

In late December, 1988, the *Wall Street Journal Europe* announced in the Money and Markets section 'West German bond traders are given new lending tool.' The German market reaction to this 'official' news of the first securities lending programme was little more than a yawn: a few telephone inquiries were received at the financial institution offering the product. Certainly the stock market crash in October, 1987 dampened interest in lending products owing to the significant decrease in trading volumes. But this hardly explains why it would take almost one and a half years before an 'official' local market lending programme organised by the central securities depository was inaugurated.

The answer lies in the fact that the major local financial institutions were digesting the basics of securities lending and starting their own securities lending task forces – but at their own pace. The bond lending programme set up by a subsidiary of a major foreign bank came as no major surprise and therefore the reaction was low-key. The practice had been observed in major markets such as the US and UK for several years. The basic economic incentives for the practice were well known. Working groups supported by local banking associations such as the 'Bundesverband der deutschen Banken' (Association of German Banks) had been examining the legal and accounting aspects of securities lending for some time. Driving this basic interest in securities lending was the securities market itself. Trading in German government bonds ('Bunds') had developed into a predominant sector of the

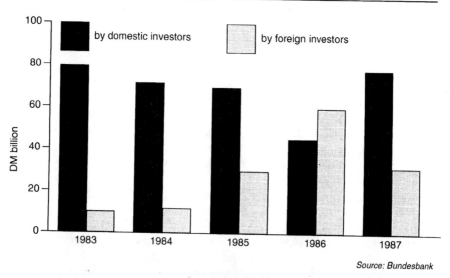

Figure 2.1: Net purchase of deutsche mark bonds.

German securities market. Trading was further stimulated by a surge in foreign professional and investor interest in 'Bunds' as indicated by Figure 2.1. As off-shore players clamoured for the opportunity to borrow Bunds the local German market responded to this foreign market demand mostly by ignoring it. Those domestic banks seeking potential sources of Bunds for lending purposes concentrated on meeting their own internal demand.

The roots of this reaction lie in several factors peculiar if not unique to the German market: the market structure and stage of development, the regulatory environment, the sophistication level of securities settlement techniques, and a traditional market reluctance to readily accept innovation without long and often painful scrutiny. Since these internal barriers have been to a large extent overcome, securities lending has been recognised as a legitimate market instrument and is currently in the state of transition from an 'accepted practice' to a commonly used financial tool.

THE LONG AND HARD ROAD TO SECURITIES LENDING 1986–1990: MAJOR MARKET FACTORS AFFECTING RAPID DEVELOPMENT

Market Structure and Stage of Development

While the US and UK markets rapidly expanded into derivative products, and other markets seeking global recognition embraced financial futures, the

German market was hampered by legal constraints and 'benign neglect'. Both regulatory authorities and the major banks, which traditionally provide directional guidance in the market, moved slowly towards development of financial futures. Certainly the necessity of amending the German stock exchange laws to avoid the liabilities under Paragraphs 762 and 764 of the German 'gambling laws' contributed to the largesse of these institutions. Margin accounts for futures transactions maintained by brokers for non-bank clients were basically defined as falling under the gambling laws. Individuals and companies could therefore sue the institution acting as their futures broker for repayment of their margins in the event that they incurred losses from futures contracts.

Financial community lobbying to amend the law to allow the rapid establishment of a futures market became lost in the politics of 'rich man versus poor man'. Initiatives to deregulate the German market through statutory amendments are often viewed by German politicians as an attempt to allow wealthy individuals and corporations to enhance their profitability at the expense of government tax receipts and those citizens not fortunate enough to participate in the benefits of a deregulated environment. Amending the stock exchange laws were viewed by the German political parties as a *heisse Kartoffel* or hot potato with significant social and political implications. This problem was compounded by debate concerning other attributes of the German market considered unfavourable for attracting both foreign and local investors: minimum reserve regulations, stock exchange turnover tax, withholding tax on dividends.

Although the gambling law problem was eventually solved in time for the Deutsche Terminboerse (DTB) to begin operations in 1990, the two-to-three year delay in establishing a futures market negatively affected efforts to develop the securities lending product. The main impetus at the major German banks for developing securities lending capabilities came from the necessity of hedging futures transactions. The start-up and success of the LIFFE Bund contract in September, 1988 certainly acted as a catalyst in establishing the DTB, but at the same time focused even more attention on securities lending as an important support product for the soon-to-be established futures market in Germany. The various internal and external securities lending working groups at the local banks synchronised their time schedules in co-ordination with the opening of the DTB.

Other immediate incentives for lending such as taking short positions, settlement efficiency, and meeting off-shore demand became secondary if not complementary. However, most major German banks had good reason not to focus on these immediate incentives: for some time most of them had already been borrowing securities from their investor clients for position-taking and settlement purposes. Through bilateral arrangements their internal needs were at least partially satisfied. Meeting foreign market demand was not deemed necessary or desirable at this point in time and therefore relegated to the proverbial 'back burner'.

Another feature of the German market affecting the pace of securities lending development came into play at this time as well: the dominance of the major German banking institutions in shaping local market change. The 'Big 3' banks, a handful of other major regional banks, and highly respected smaller specialised institutions typically set the trends and examples for the market as a whole. The influence of the 'universal bank' (i.e. consolidated commercial and investment banking capabilities) on local market investors and the actions of all other banks in the market-place should not be underestimated. The sheer market-making power of the leading German banks can directly affect the introduction of a new banking product in the market. The risk of limited success or outright failure of a new product not ingratiated by the leading institutions often stymies the introduction of new products.

The development of securities lending in Germany was slowed by the attitude of the leading banks towards the product as described above. The fate of securities lending programmes was thus linked directly to the establishment of a futures market with its inherent delays. The creation of securities lending programmes by banks outside the 'inner circle' of German banks was also affected. Limited success was predestined for these programmes as market acceptance would be minimal without the endorsement of the leading local institutions.

Regulatory Environment

The regulatory situation in the German market has not been very conducive to establishing securities lending programmes. Since 1986, few changes have occurred to improve the situation. In January, 1990 the stock exchange turnover tax for equities lending in the local market was abolished, thereby paving the way for increased equities lending activity. As previously mentioned, the stock exchange laws were also amended to avoid the implications of the gambling law and allow the establishment of the DTB in early 1990. Prior to these events, the abolition of the short-lived, ill-fated (and ill-conceived!) withholding tax on fixed income instruments in June, 1989 was the only regulatory change that affected securities lending capability. Although damage had already been done to investor interest in 'Bunds', the potential for restoring faith in the Bund was enhanced by this amendment. Other major regulatory constraints still remained in place: minimum reserve requirements and controls on insurance company as well as mutual fund lending abilities. These problems are examined in more detail in the 'future prospects' section of this chapter.

A major change related to the regulatory environment that has occurred in the market during the past five years was in the interpretation of the German Custody Law related to securities lending. The law states that one cannot trade an undeliverable position, i.e., a security sale without the ability to deliver the security is not allowed. The intent of this regulation is to prevent unhedged short positions and potential financial losses. There is no reference to ownership of the deliverable security or borrowing a security to meet a delivery. Since the concept of borrowing securities was relatively foreign to the German market, it was always assumed that securities delivered to meet the conditions of a trade were by definition securities owned by the delivering party. The concept of 'going short' was therefore interpreted as being forbidden in the German market. In reality securities lending fulfils the stipulations of the law by allowing deliveries to be made even if the securities are not owned by the seller. It was therefore not surprising that initial lending programmes established in the market received a 'nod' or unofficial approval from the Bundesbank.

As securities lending programmes evolved, the 'can't go short' interpretation was still widely held in the market – even among professionals. As more institutions studied the legal aspects of securities lending in more detail in preparation for the futures market, this interpretation lost credibility. However, it still made its contribution to the slow acceptance of securities lending in the market.

Level of Securities Settlement Techniques

One of the major factors that produced lethargy towards securities lending in the domestic banks was the lack of communication between the front office (traders, dealers) and the back office (settlement departments). It can be argued that the sheer size of these operations at the major German banks prevent effective communications. But at the same time the size of the market makers' volume practically demanded that some effort be made to link settlement costs to trading profitability. Many of the trading groups of market makers worked in 'splendid isolation' with little concern for the level of back office efficiency in settling their trades. Minimal time was lost reflecting on the 'all-in' profitability of a trade when securities were not delivered on time. The general opinion among traders was that if a delivery was delayed, the costs were probably compensated by the savings on delayed purchases. If one was an active trader or market maker, then over time costs would be netted by savings. In defence of German banks, the same situation existed at the major US and UK broker/dealers until after the stock market crash in 1987.

Compounding this problem was the inherent one-day financing cost when settling through the Kassenverein (KV) system in the German market. The overnight batch processing methods and limited automation of this central depository made it virtually impossible to settle a back-to-back trade through the standard settlement process. KV members fully accepted the inevitability of one day's financing costs in the market. Little time was spent exploring means of settling back-to-back trades by utilising securities lending or other innovative means.

The concept of 'settlement management' was hardly recognised until as late as 1990. This concept uses securities lending and 'forced deliveries' (pre-matching of receipt and delivery instructions) to achieve same day turnaround and accelerate cash flow.

A limited number of banks have experimented with settlement management techniques since a high level of settlements automation is required. Securities positions and delivery and receipt orders have to be known early in the day to enable pre-matching or delivery of borrowed securities. Most German banks have been improving their automation to meet the demands of the same day settlement environment expected at the end of the first quarter of 1992 with the *Kassenverein Neu* or the New Kassenverein. Owing to the considerable systems requirements of this KV modernisation programme, most banks have had limited time to implement settlement management techniques, despite the interest savings that can be achieved. Many have simply waited for the KV Neu to deliver improved efficiency.

The slow recognition of the linkage between trading profits and settlement costs, as well as the lack of more sophisticated settlement techniques to avoid KV settlement inefficiency, certainly constrained the practice of securities lending in the German market. The strong desire currently exhibited by banks to improve settlement efficiency and to benefit from the KV Neu should act as a catalyst for the further development of securities lending in Germany.

Reluctance to Readily Accept Innovation

A final underlying factor that negatively affected the development of securities lending in the German market must be ascribed to the general conservative attitude of domestic institutions towards innovation. Time-tried methods are the accepted norm in the market. New instruments or products are often met with strong resistance by the clients of the local banks, which then reinforces the sceptical attitude of the banks themselves towards new ideas. Successful innovation in foreign markets is not necessarily viewed as sensible for the German market. Demands or pressure from foreign investors and global players have limited influence on market acceptance of new products. The focus is clearly on the local market first, then in relation to the rest of the world. This is not an unusual situation: many European markets react in the same way. However, some other 'less important' European markets have embraced internal and external innovation with far less hesitation than the German market. The importance of this traditional resistance to change should not be overestimated when considering the fate of securities lending in Germany, but should be recognised as having reinforced the major barriers to development.

MAJOR MARKET DEVELOPMENTS IN 1990: SECURITIES LENDING FINALLY ESTABLISHED AS A VIABLE PRODUCT

Existing Programmes and the Start of the DTB

By 1990, a limited number of securities lending initiatives had been undertaken by individual banks in the market-place, mainly for in-house purposes. J.P. Morgan GmbH introduced the first lending programme for Bunds in April, 1988 followed six months later by Bobls (*Bundesobligationen*) and finally by the DAX equities in November, 1989. Morgan borrowed securities under contract from client portfolios and used them for its own trading book and for securities clearing and custody client settlements. Other institutions in the market also began setting up their own programmes, usually for in-house purposes. But the momentum to establish securities lending as a real market tool was still lacking.

The needed impulse was provided by the delayed opening in January 1990 of the Deutsche Terminboerse (DTB), the German financial futures and options exchange. The DTB was officially founded in the summer of 1988. The amendment to Article 22 of the Capital Transaction Tax Law to exempt options trading and securities lending from the stock exchange turnover tax, as well as the amendment to Paragraph 53 of the stock exchange law to avoid gambling regulations, was necessary to pave the way for the DTB's first product – stock options on 14 stocks of the DAX (Deutsche Aktien Index). Options trading in turn generated immediate incentive among the participating institutions to borrow securities.

As noted previously, domestic banks timed their development of securities lending with the start of the DTB. Many had gained experience in futures through the LIFFE 'Bund' contract in London and recognised that a decent cash and carry arbitrage could only be achieved by borrowing securities and delivering them to cover one's position when the futures contract expired. Trading options on the DTB required a liquid securities borrowing source in order to perfect 'delta hedge' transactions, an important risk-inhibiting method in successful options trading. Most of the German banks' interest in securities lending remains focused on borrowing for one's own position-taking on the DTB.

Inauguration of the Kassenverein Programme

On 7 June 1990 the Kassenverein 'legitimised' the status of securities lending by commencing a lending programme with the 30 DAX index shares. This was anxiously awaited by its members and by the trading community. In August, 1990 the KV programme was expanded to include the Bunds. At this point in time, doubts about the legal and regulatory aspects of securities lending in Germany were dispelled and it finally became established among the German banking community as a viable product.

CURRENT STATUS OF SECURITIES LENDING IN GERMANY: THE DEUTSCHER KASSENVEREIN SYSTEM

Linkage to the Futures Market

In November, 1990 the DTB started trading two futures contracts, namely the Bund and the DAX index. The Bund future is almost identical to the LIFFE Bund contract with one major difference: the LIFFE contract is traded in a 'pit' on an open outcry basis while the DTB contract is traded on a computer exchange, as is the DAX futures contract.

Volumes on the DTB Bund contract were initially very low in comparison to the LIFFE contract. Computer hardware problems that led to time delays in keying in orders and receiving trade confirmations hampered the first six months of the contract's life. From November, 1990 to April, 1991 the average daily number of contracts were around 3,800 compared to 30,000 for the LIFFE contract. Experts were questioning the viability of the DTB Bund contract. The situation changed dramatically in the second half of 1991 when the computer hardware problems were solved (allowing trades to be input and confirmed in less than half a second) and the DTB decided to eliminate fees for the contract. In addition, major German futures traders, namely the large banks, instructed their traders to move business from LIFFE to the DTB in November, 1991, which gave a huge boost to contract volumes. This is reflected in Figure 2.2 as well as the rapid increase in contract volume to an average of over 190,000 contracts per month or 9,000 per day. In comparison, the average number of LIFFE contracts in 1991 was more than 40,000. Presently LIFFE contract volumes tend to be three times the DTB volumes on hectic trading days while contract volumes are approximately 60 per cent of the LIFFE contract on normal business days. The DTB DAX futures contract volumes also increased throughout 1991, but at a considerably slower pace than Bund volumes.

DTB options trading performed more consistently and substantially better than the futures contracts. Options trading has enjoyed the benefits of a

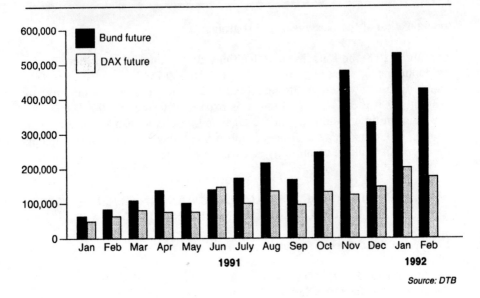

Figure 2.2: DTB financial futures – contract volume.

longer existence and market volatility along with the uncertainties of the Gulf War as seen in Figure 2.3.

Development of securities lending in the German market is closely linked to the success of the domestic options and futures market. It is expected that securities lending in the domestic German market will grow in step with DTB trading volumes. This prognosis has been confirmed in an article in the respected German financial daily the *Handelsblatt* in February, 1991, which also announced that the German market has accepted securities lending. The options and futures market in Germany has not been in existence long enough to predict its medium and long-term success, but clearly it has not grown as quickly as the founders hoped or fast enough to give securities lending programmes the momentum needed for full development.

The Framework for the Kassenverein's Securities Lending Programme

To better understand how the KV's securities lending programme functions and the role that the KV plays in the securities market, it is worth devoting some time describing the organisation and structure of the institution. The KV is Germany's central securities depository and as such a bank with a restricted business licence. For example, the KV is not allowed to engage in the extension of loans, deposit taking, securities underwriting or advising on

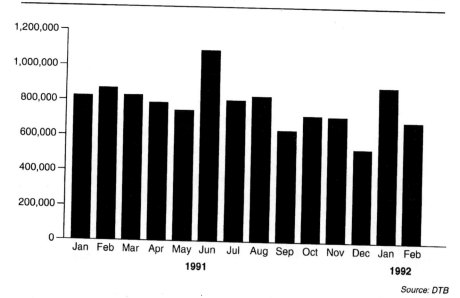

Figure 2.3 *DTB Stock options – contract volume.*

investments. It is subject to control by the Federal Banking Supervisory Office (*Bundesaufsichtsamt*) in Berlin as all banks are in Germany. However, the KV also had to apply for additional authorisation from the Federal state or states in which it is operating in order to obtain the status of a central depository.

The mandate of the KV is to provide safe custody and clearing of securities for its member banks and to settle securities trades transacted through the stock exchange. The settlement of securities transfers between account holders are handled on a book entry, against payment or free-of-payment basis. Supporting services related to securities settlement, such as interest/dividend payments and corporate actions, are also provided. The KV itself, however, does not exercise voting rights. The KV holds over 19,000 various securities in collective safe custody with 90 per cent consisting of fixed income instruments. Over 19.5 million book entry transfers with some DEM 2.8 trillion worth of DVP transfers were processed by the KV in 1990. Substantial support for this huge administrative burden is supplied by a KV subsidiary called the *Deutsche Wertpapierdaten-Zentrale GmbH* (**DWZ**) or German Securities Data Centre, which is a data processing company that acts as the central bookkeeping arm of the KV. The DWZ also offers securities data services such as position reporting directly to KV members.

The KV's membership at the end of 1991 consisted of some 576 banks. It should be noted that there is increasing pressure on the KV to allow insurance companies, corporations and financial funds to be eligible for membership. The KV's shareholders, 75 domestic banks holding the KV's capital of DEM 22 million, are certainly not enthusiastic about expanding the membership to non-banks since these new members could hold their securities assets directly at the KV rather than through a local bank. This potential loss of business for the bank members has stalled the expansion of membership, but as the non-bank institutions expand more into the banking field (by buying into banks, for example), the eventual admission of non-bank members is inevitable. The consolidation of the Kassenverein system in Germany, which was completed by the end of 1989, was a significant milestone in the future direction of the system. Until that time, there were seven legally independent Kassenvereine operating in the major German cities where stock exchanges exist, namely Berlin, Dusseldorf, Frankfurt, Hamburg, Hanover, Munich and Stuttgart.

A major effort was undertaken to form one national institution that would be legally and technically merged to provide securities settlement and cost efficiencies. This task appeared easier said than done, as the shareholders of some of the various Kassenvereine consisted not only of banks, but of the state or city-state they were located in. The proposed consolidation took on political overtones as some Kassenvereine feared the loss of their independence.

This attitude was not entirely unjustified since the Frankfurter Kassenverein was by far the predominant securities settling institution with well over 50 per cent of the total volume in Germany and would certainly set the pace in a merged institution. Since each Kassenverein had taken rather independent decisions on the systems hardware/software they utilised, many of the processing systems were incompatible, which led to considerable debate about which systems would be made redundant and which would survive. This certainly fuelled the merger controversy.

However, in the end common sense prevailed against regional animosities and the 'Deutscher Kassenverein AG', with its main office in Frankfurt, was formed with branch offices operating in the same premises as the former Kassenvereine. This completed merger enabled major steps to be taken towards modernisation of the KV system and the establishment of a KV securities lending programme.

Securities Lending as an Integral Part of the Modernisation of the KV

The securities lending programme of the KV is one of the major projects completed or being undertaken to modernise the German securities clearing system. The changes currently taking place represent the most significant alterations in the Kassenverein system since its formation in the 1920s and the establishment of the first central securities depository in Germany in 1882, which was located in Berlin. In November, 1991 Phase I of the 'Kassenverein Neu' or 'New Kassenverein' was partially implemented. Same day settlement (SDS) processing became possible but dependent upon the number of banks voluntarily matching orders through the *Cascade* system. SDS volumes were minimal since few KV members participated in SDS initially as they were waiting for further Phase I developments. Phase I is expected to be completed in the second quarter of 1992 when matching will become obligatory and inquiry capabilities through *Cascade* are made available. Volumes should then be substantial as same day turnaround of back-to-back securities trades will become more efficient, thereby eliminating one day financing costs due to the KV's previous overnight processing standards.

In Phases II and III of the KV Neu, which should be completed by the end of 1993, improvements such as transaction chaining, contract note automation, primary market settlement, and real time settlement of transactions are planned. KV Neu is aimed at establishing the German securities settlement system as one of the premier settlement systems in the world financial markets, not excluding Euroclear and Cedel. It is intended that the Group of 30 recommendations for securities settlement be at least met and in some cases exceeded. The KV's securities lending programme is considered to be an important part of KV Neu and its future.

How the KV Securities Lending Programme Functions

First it is important to note that the programme is designed only for KV members who have signed the borrowing and lending agreements. Non-banks and international banks and brokers are not eligible to directly lend or borrow from the KV. Non-members need to borrow or lend through a member bank, which will exact a fee for providing access to the programme. As a securities clearing and collective safe custody bank, the KV acts as a trustee in its lending programme – not as a principal. In this regard the KV programme is similar to the established lending programmes of the international clearing institutions like Euroclear and Cedel, which act as agents but provide indemnification through a guarantee from a bank or consortium of banks.

The KV assigns a unique reference number to each lending transaction and guarantees anonymity of borrower and lender by not disclosing the borrower's name to the lender. Automatic and opportunity lenders designate their lendable securities to a lending pool in the KV from which the KV

International Securities Lending

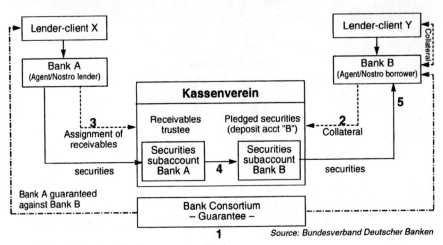

1. Bank Consortium guarantee for emergency situations
2. Collateral supplied before securities are delivered
3. The KV assigns collateral to the lender
4. Borrowed securities credited to Bank B subaccount
5. Securities available to borrower on value date

Figure 2.4: Kassenverein securities lending programme structure

allocates demand to its individual borrowers. There is no automatic borrowing as with the Euroclear and Cedel programmes. An automatic lender transfers securities intended for the programme to a KV subaccount in the lender's name and these securities are automatically included in the daily allotment of securities available for lending. If borrowing demand cannot be met by the supply of securities from the automatic lenders, the opportunity lenders are then approached by the KV. The KV matches the borrowing requests and lending supply as early as possible in the programme's timeframe with borrowing priorities set by objective criteria and a random generator.

Since the KV has a limited capital base of DEM 22 million, a bank guarantee consortium consisting of 20 KV member banks was established to provide financial support in the event of an emergency (refer to Figure 2.4 to follow the KV programme structure). If a borrower goes bankrupt and the collateral value (as marked to market daily by the KV) does not fully cover the value of the securities borrowed, the consortium will make up the difference. Borrowers are protected from a bankrupt lender by the collateral they have pledged to the KV, which will be returned when the lending transaction is concluded. The consortium guarantee totals DEM 50 million with the provision to increase the guarantee amount accordingly if the daily outstandings of the lending programme exceed DEM 3 trillion (DEM 3000 billion).

Borrowers need to notify the KV of their intention to borrow between 8 a.m. and 4 p.m. Frankfurt Local Time (FLT) one day prior to the value date of the borrowing. Lenders need to inform the KV of their intention to recall securities from the lending programme between 8 a.m. and 12 noon FLT for value in five days. The borrower also has to provide collateral to the KV in the amount of 100 per cent of market value for equities and 105 per cent for fixed income securities one day prior to the borrowing. Acceptable collateral is either a non-interest bearing cash deposit (DEM and valued at 100 per cent) placed with the Landeszentralbank (LZB – local office of the Bundesbank) or a pledge to the KV on a separate pledge account of German fixed income securities (valued at 90 per cent of market value) or equities (valued at 80 per cent of market value). Since the KV acts as a trustee, the pledged securities are then assigned to the lending bank. Only after sufficient collateral has been pledged to the KV are the borrowed securities allocated to the borrower's account with the KV.

Thus it is only late in the afternoon prior to value date that the borrower actually knows whether or not a borrowing request will be filled fully, partially or not at all. On value date the borrower is free to dispose of the borrowed securities as desired. A lender to the KV programme may recall securities with five stock exchange business days' notice. Recall notices must be communicated to the KV before 12 noon FLT. Should the borrower fail to return the borrowed securities by the fifth day of the recall period, the KV uses the collateral provided by the borrower to execute a buy-in on the following day. If the collateral is not sufficient to execute a buy-in, the bank consortium provides the difference. As far as redeliveries are concerned, a borrower may return borrowed securities by informing the KV up to 4 p.m. FLT one day prior to redelivery date.

Securities, Fees and Lending Limits

Over 160 fixed income securities including the most recent ten year government bond issues (*Bunds*), 2–6 year medium-term government notes (*Bundesschätzanweisungen*), and five year special government notes (*Bundesobligationen* or '*Bobls*') are eligible fixed income instruments for the KV lending programme. There are over 60 eligible equities, including the 30 DAX (Deutsche Aktien-Index or German Stock Index) stocks excluding Allianz shares, which are registered shares and settled physically. It should be noted that the KV is continuously expanding the list of eligible securities for their lending programme. Borrowing fees paid to the lender are calculated inclusively from the first lending day to the day preceding the return transfer of securities. Standard fees for the borrower amount to a fixed 3 per cent p.a. for equities and 2.25 per cent for bonds with a minimum of DEM 160. The lender receives a 2.5 per cent p.a. fee for equities and 1.75 per cent for bonds with a minimum of DEM 130. The guarantee consortium receives a ¼ per cent fee, minimum DEM 15, which is deducted from the fixed fee paid by the borrower.

The KV also receives a fee of ¼ per cent with a minimum DEM 15 for processing costs. Certain lending limits have also been placed on borrowers under the KV programme. To begin with, a borrow may last no longer than six months. The maximum amount of a security available at one time for lending is limited to 10 per cent of the holdings of the share capital for stocks and 10 per cent of the total issue for fixed income securities. In addition, a borrower may borrow up to 10 per cent of the maximum available total for a security, i.e. 1 per cent of share capital and 1 per cent of an issue. A borrower is also limited to borrowing securities up to 50 per cent of his own share capital. An overview of the major parameters of the KV lending programme are listed in Table 2.1.

Positive and Negative Aspects of the KV Lending Programme

Securities lending at the KV takes place in a very safe environment, which is operated by settlement professionals and backed by a strong banking consortium. Since securities lending takes place on strictly a DVP and fully collateralised basis, the programme continues the KV tradition of protecting the end investor or in the case of securities lending, the lender. It is also important to remember that the KV programme was designed for the domestic environment and has contributed to the further development of securities lending in the German market by placing an 'imprimatur' on the concept of securities lending through its inception alone. At the same time, the rest of the lending world has scrutinised the KV programme and discovered that there are several prohibitive elements. The most striking weakness of the programme are the high minimum fees for borrowers. The total amount adds up to a minimum of DEM 160 per lending transaction. For most borrowers, this minimum fee is too high. In addition to this problem, the KV programme does not pay interest on a borrower's cash collateral. This is contrary to lending programmes in several other markets where the economic viability of securities lending is dependent upon cash collateral earning interest at market rates. In defence of the KV, one should note that cash collateral is on deposit at the LZB, the local arm of the Bundesbank. The LZB's policy has always been negative towards paying any interest on excess balances or cash collateral. The KV has limited influence over this Bundesbank policy.

If we more closely examine the KV programme, we find several other 'undesirable' conditions that do not contribute to utilisation of the programme. The lending limits imposed severely restrict the total in one line of

		Equities	Bonds	Minimum
Eligible lenders/borrowers:	Banks which are KV participants			
Fees:	Borrower fixed:	3%	2.25%	DM 160.00
	Lender fixed:	2.5%	1.75%	DM 130.00
	Guarantee consortium fixed:	0.25%	0.25%	DM 15.00
	KV service charge:	0.25%	0.25%	DM 15.00
Lendable securities:	Over 160 Bunds, Kassen, Bobls, rail and port issues; over 60 German equities, including the DAX-index (excluding Allianz)			
Collateral eligible:	Cash, DEM securities (no interest on cash)			
Collateral required:	100% of market value (equities borrowed) 100% of market value (bonds borrowed)			
Collateral valuation:	80% of market value (equities pledged) 90% of market value (bonds pledged)			
Recall period:	5 days notice (exchange business days)			
Deadlines:	Borrowers: from 8:00a.m. to 4:00p.m. for next day value Lenders: from 8:00a.m. to 12:00p.m. for recall five days value			
Lending limits:	Max. total available	10% of share capital or of issue amount		
	Max. total per borrower:	a) 10% of total available b) 50% of borrower's capital		
	Max. lending period	6 months		

Table 2.1: Kassenverein Lending Overview

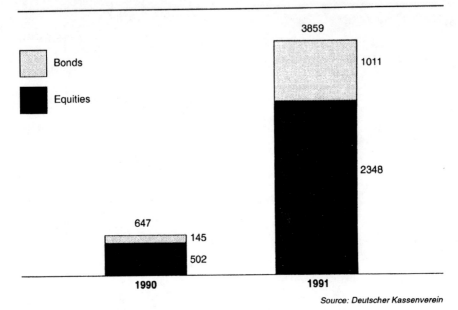

Figure 2.5: Kassenverein transaction volume

securities to be borrowed by any one single borrower. Low capitalised borrowers are also restricted in the amount of securities they can borrow, despite their pledge of collateral. Foreign bank subsidiaries, which are usually active users of borrowing programmes, are particularly restrained by this requirement as most of them are capitalised between DEM 25 and 100 million.

Other weaknesses in the KV programme that should be noted are: fixed rates unrelated to market demand, no term borrowing, no borrowing reservations, no immediate answer on availability of borrowed securities.

If we look at the success of the KV lending programme after its first eighteen months in operation (see Figure 2.5), we find substantially increased volumes in 1991 compared to 1990: from 5 to 15 daily transactions on average. These volumes are still relatively weak compared with other programmes in the local market and especially with lending volumes in developed markets such as the U.S. and the U.K. Contributing to the low volumes in the KV programme are the small number of participants. In January, 1992, there were only 56 lenders and 45 borrowers. Still less than 10 per cent of the KV members are users of the lending programme.

However, the major positive aspects of the KV securities lending programme should not be ignored: growing volume due to increasing participant interest and the commitment of the KV to adjust the programme to accommodate market interests over time. The DKV is cognisant of the programme's weaknesses and is taking steps to correct them. A time factor is involved, but we can expect to see a shift towards more standard securities lending conditions in the programme's structure going forward.

THE CURRENT STATUS OF SECURITIES LENDING IN GERMANY: ALTERNATIVES TO THE KV LENDING PROGRAMME

Commercial Bank Programmes

Outside of the formal lending programmes offered for German securities by Euroclear and Cedel, local banks in the German market are also active borrowers and lenders of DEM securities. Several institutions offer lending programmes that cater to foreign programme users in addition to their own domestic use. The banks typically mentioned in the German press and known to be conducting active lending programmes in the market are BHF Bank, Bank of Tokyo, Deutsche Bank, Dresdner Bank and J.P. Morgan. Increasingly more major regional banks and *Landesbanken* (state central banks) are establishing their own programmes. Major broker/dealers such as Goldman Sachs, Merrill Lynch, Morgan Stanley, Salomon Brothers and Shearson Lehman Brothers are less active in the German market as they prefer to handle their international securities lending and repo business out of London.

The parameters of the local bank programmes are very similar, with a structure more resembling international lending programme standards (see Figure 2.6). To begin with, a wider range of securities are eligible for these

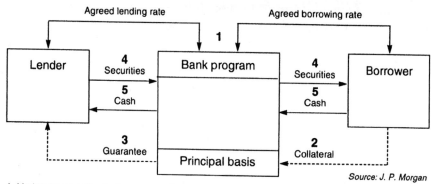

1. Market driven or fixed rates are negotiated
2. Collateral must be available when securities credited to borrower's account
3. If required, lender receives guarantee based on collateral
4. Securities from lender are credited to borrower's account
5. Borrower pays agreed rate at close of borrow or receives monthly statement; lender receives statement rate on monthly basis

Figure 2.6: OTC securities lending programme structure

programmes, both for equities and fixed income securities. Bunds and Bobls include older issues, and non-DAX equities are in all programmes. Eligibility is driven by demand, so if a borrower is seeking a large order of an obscure stock, most of the bank programmes will try to accommodate the borrower. To this extent even the physically handled Allianz shares are made available to borrowers.

Borrowing and lending fees are also market driven. Although some programmes set an internal fixed rate target, flexible pricing is the standard practice depending on availability and demand. Borrowers typically pay between 1–3 per cent p.a. for fixed income securities and between 2–4 per cent p.a. for equities. Lenders receive between ½–1½ per cent p.a. for fixed income and 1–2 per cent for equities. Minimum fees vary from zero to DEM 250. Recall periods typically correspond to the international and KV standard of five business days, although some programmes set a notice of return period for the borrower of one to three days. Deadlines for placing borrowing orders are usually up to 12 noon one day prior to settlement date, but this deadline can often be moved back to as late as 3 p.m. on a case-to-case and 'best efforts' basis.

The limitations for borrowers tend to be more flexible than the KV programme. Typically the maximum borrowing period is open, except for one programme that upholds the six month limit of the KV programme. Term borrowing is included in most of the programmes as is the possibility of reserving or earmarking potential borrowings. Maximum borrowing amounts are set by about one third of the programmes.

Collateral requirements are also more flexible. Bank guarantees or standby letters of credit are accepted as collateral, in addition to cash and securities. The banks act on a principal basis in their programmes rather than on a trustee or agent basis, and are therefore always the counterparty to the lenders and borrowers. In effect, the banks become the legal owner of securities borrowed from a lender. The lender's risk is the bank and not the borrower, while the bank's risk is the borrower. Collateral plays an important role in securing the bank's risk, while the credit standing of the bank is decisive for the lender. An excellent credit standing is required in the German market in order to set up a successful lending programme. Collateral is valued along the same lines as the KV programme. Borrowers also receive interest at market rates on cash used as collateral. This makes cash a more attractive means of collateralisation, except for the nearly 100 basis points lost as a result of the minimum reserve regulations where applicable.

An overview of the typical bank lending programme is provided in Table 2.2. Clearly, the bank programmes are considerably more flexible, less expensive, and provide more options than the KV programme. Clearly the necessity of providing a service that is competitive with the offshore lending programmes has formed the structure of the bank programmes and will be the guiding force as the market and programmes continue to develop.

Repo Market

As a cheaper alternative to securities lending the repo market is often used by traders doing longer-term arbitrage. A repo market has been established in Germany, but is structured differently than most repo markets. The only 'real' repos (i.e., 'American style' where cheap financing is the goal) done in Germany are transacted directly between the banks and the Bundesbank. The driving force behind these repos is the desire of the banks to access cheap funding by going to the Lombard window of the Bundesbank in times of tight money supply or unforeseeable cash clearing overdrafts. Other than for these reasons, the repo in the standard sense is not a frequently used vehicle in the German market. In fact, a repo market in the American sense is openly discouraged by the Bundesbank and is subject to the minimum reserve regulations, which make such repos economically unviable as a financing instrument.

Another breed of repo has developed which basically works as a buy/sell-back with the 'borrowing fee' calculated in the forward price. The driving force of this type of repo is to acquire specific securities cheaply rather than raise cheap financing. In turn, the lender of the securities requires cash collateral on which interest is paid at market rates less the borrowing spread. The borrower buys spot and sells back forward with only two tickets written on the same trade date with different value dates. The securities borrowed via this type of repo are typically delivered on to the market.

The securities returned on the forward date are of the same type, amount and quality but not the exact same securities purchased initially. Repo rates in this market are much more flexible than the lending market, usually in larger amounts, and the bid/offer spreads often are somewhat wider than in the cash market. None of the players in the market really run a 'matched book', since one is never sure at what rates and how fast one can sell the stock coming in through a reverse repo. The few players in this market regard the instrument primarily as an additional source or outlet of securities for their lending efforts.

The greatest liquidity in repos is still in the London market. Less than a handful of broker firms are crossing the Channel and matching counterparties on a name give-up basis. This will only change when the minimum reserve requirements of the Bundesbank are lifted off repos. Only at this time will repos find broad acceptance in the market and stimulate the establishment of an industry-wide repo agreement similar to the PSA agreement. For now repos in the German market are not a legitimate alternative to securities

Eligible lenders/borrowers:	Domestic and international investors, banks, broker/dealers
Fees:	Borrower: variable −1% to −3% fixed income −2% to −4% equities, min. DEM 0 – 250
	Lender variable: +½% to 1½% fixed income +1% to 2% equities
Lendable securities:	Bunds
	Bobls
	Dax index shares + non-DAX
Collateral eligible:	Cash, securities or guarantee (interest on cash)
Collateral required:	110% of market value (equities borrowed)
	105% of market value (bonds borrowed)
Collateral valuation:	50% of market value (equities pledged)
	75% of market value (bonds pledged)
Recall period:	4–5 days notice (exchange business days)
Deadlines:	Borrowers: from 8:00a.m. to 12:00p.m. for next day value (exceptions at 3:00p.m.)
	Lenders: from 8:00a.m. to 12:00p.m. for recall four to five days value
Lending limits:	Max. total available: Depends on program size/availability
	Max. total per borrower: ⅔rds of program; no limits
	Max. lending period: Open (some 6 months)

Table 2.2: Bank Program Lending Overview

lending, although the use of the unique German instrument is growing in terms of volume and participants.

LEGAL AND ACCOUNTING ASPECTS

Under German law the borrower becomes the legal owner of the borrowed securities and may use them for whatever purpose deemed necessary. Economic ownership, however, remains with the lender (beneficial holder) who is entitled to receive compensation for all cash and non-cash benefits as well as rights arising from the securities. The only right passed on with lent stock is the voting right, which can be exercised once per year at the annual shareholders meeting.

From an accounting point of view it is important to note that securities lending does not result in the realisation of hidden reserves. It is not the lender's intention to permanently dispose of the securities but rather to 'pass' them on temporarily and make them available for alternative usage. For the duration of the loan the lender reduces his asset position under the balance sheet position 'Own Securities' and books the borrower's obligation to return the securities under the position 'Accounts Receivable' with exactly the same book value. The overall result is that there is a change in the asset composition of the balance sheet, but no change in the balance sheet total.

On the other hand, the borrower books the borrowed securities under the position 'Own Securities' at market value. A corresponding amount has to be booked under 'Liabilities' (i.e., the borrower's obligation to return the securities) with the result that the borrower's balance sheet will grow by the market value of the borrowed securities position.

Overall, the legal aspects of securities lending in Germany is relatively straightforward with the legal basis embodied in Paragraph 607 and attachments of the German Civil Code. It should be noted that a securities lending and borrowing agreement governs the details of securities lending transactions in Germany. There is no standard agreement accepted in the market, but most are similarly structured. One important aspect of these agreements are the provisions for stock loans extended over the dividend date. German tax law, in seeking to avoid double taxation, provides a tax credit only to the domestic shareholder which brings the effective amount of the dividend received to 156.25 per cent. This means that domestic and international borrowers of securities over the dividend date need to reimburse the bona fide owner of the shares DEM 156.25 for every DEM 100 worth of dividend. The only time that this situation does not apply is when the lender and borrower of the securities are offshore. The possibility of matching international borrowers and lenders in domestic lending programmes is very limited due to the structure of the lending pools.

REQUIRED CHANGES AND FUTURE PROSPECTS FOR SECURITIES LENDING IN GERMANY

Since the establishment of the KV lending programme in June, 1990, German domestic interest in securities lending has been growing steadily, although no rapid expansion in the business has taken place yet. Foreign interest has been strong for the last three to four years with demand being met mainly by supply from off-shore lenders rather than from the local German market. An increasing number of domestic banks have become involved in securities lending. A few banks have set up 'full service' programmes, but most of the banks involved in any significant form of securities trading have established proprietary programmes. With this scenario alone, growth in securities lending is expected. However, the pace of the growth is dependent upon several changes and enhancements that need to occur in the market. Without at least some of these changes taking place, there will not be significant growth in the business.

Regulatory Changes

The major road block to a fully developed securities lending market in Germany is the minimum reserve policy of the Bundesbank. According to the minimum reserve regulations, all cash deposits with German banks from domestic non-banks and foreign depositors are subject to the regulation. This applies to deposits held as cash collateral for securities borrowings as well as for repos. The amount that has to be kept in an interest free deposit with the Bundesbank varies by maturity. The banks have to report their deposits by maturity four times per month. At the end of each month the Bundesbank indicates the average minimum reserve requirement to be kept the following month. It is at the discretion of each individual bank to decide how they meet the minimum reserve requirement in the course of each month, i.e. at the beginning, in the middle or end of the month or on average during the month.

For deposits with maturities up to 30 days, 12.1 per cent must be held in the interest free Bundesbank account; for deposits with maturities from 31 days to four years, 4.65 per cent must be held. Assuming a theoretical deposit rate of 9 per cent, the 12.1 per cent reserves that must be held for a deposit under one month result in a reduction in the deposit rate of 109 basis points to 7.91 per cent! This is simply too expensive for borrowers of securities holding cash collateral in Germany since it challenges the economic viability of securities lending transactions.

Will the Bundesbank alter its minimum reserve policy? The answer is somewhat obscure as the Bundesbank management itself is split into two different camps. Those Directors supporting the status quo maintain that the minimum reserve regulation has been an effective tool for controlling a tight money market policy. They argue that the benefit of the minimum reserve policy is to provide the Bundesbank with a gauge to measure the relative liquidity of the money markets, rather than the benefit lying in the instrument itself. The relative stability of the minimum reserve rates over time reflects this. Therefore, they see no need to change a proven policy.

The more dynamic directors maintain that the high level of minimum reserves required is not necessary to continue to measure the liquidity of the money market. Since banks avoid interest free deposits, are required to keep a percentage of their deposits with the Bundesbank interest free anyway, and have to meet the targets by month end, the 'gauge' always indicates a tight money supply at the end of the month when banks tend to meet the reserve targets. Under these circumstances, a considerably lower minimum reserve requirement would provide the same measurement benefits to the Bundesbank.

Presently the chances that the minimum reserve requirements are completely dropped are minimal. There is a slight chance that certain instruments, such as securities lending and repos, may be declared exempt from the regulation. Despite the fact that recent newspaper articles indicate that the Bundesbank is well aware of the fact that the regulation is acting as a brake on the rapid development of a number of financial instruments, not just securities lending, the most likely scenario is one of lower reserve requirements. Unfortunately, there is no predictable time frame and there is no immediate relief for repo product development, nor for improving the economics of cash collateral for securities borrowers.

The Bundesbank needs to realise that international holders and borrowers of German securities will stay offshore unless they feel comfortable with the collateral provided and with the level of interest on cash collateral. A large percentage of DEM securities are traded outside Germany by international market makers. At the same time foreign futures exchanges successfully offer contracts on German securities. If the Bundesbank truly supports the efforts to bring more trading back to the domestic exchanges, stronger support has to be exhibited for financial instruments widely accepted in other foreign markets. This support could be manifested in the Bundesbank taking the necessary steps to remove the inherent regulatory barriers in the German markets.

Deregulation of Major Institutional Investors

Insurance companies and mutual funds are highly regulated by their industry watchdogs, which provides for a high level of safety but few opportunities for the industry. Some of these limitations are directed at the nature and utilisation of assets, including the use of a securities portfolio for securities lending purposes. At the beginning of 1991 the law governing the insurance industry was amended to allow insurance companies to invest up to 5 per cent of their restricted assets in a wider range of investments. Additionally, they were allowed to begin lending securities. This certainly is a move in the right direction, but only a cautious step. Presently only a dozen or so insurance companies are lending a portion of their portfolios to borrowers. The number needs to grow in order to increase the liquidity of the securities lending market in Germany.

The industry regulators have not been at the forefront of new product developments because they have not regarded this as their job. The insurance companies themselves have been hesitant in exploring the potential for using the product and as a result few have a thorough understanding of the benefits, risks, structure, accounting and administrative aspects. The industry itself must devote the time to informing themselves about the details of securities lending. The operators of securities lending programmes will also have to concentrate more on marketing the product to these institutional investors.

Establishing the 'Missing Link'

Traditionally the gap between the front and back offices in German banks runs long and deep. The traders complete their trades during the business day and calculate their profit and loss every evening before leaving for the pub. They generally could not care less as to what happens in the settlements area. The fact is that the money that can be lost through settlement problems can easily nullify the profit on a trade making the daily P & L calculations of the trader less meaningful. Only a few banks in Germany have managed to bridge this gap or establish the badly needed 'missing link' between the front and back offices by appointing personnel to watch after each trade and manage the settlement, rather than simply settle a trade.

Only very few banks in the market have installed financing desks in their trading areas which are responsible for financing the traders' long and short positions. A borrowing fee is charged on all short positions and the cash is invested at market rates. At the end of each day each trader receives a report indicating the revenues actually made by that trader through the investment of cash, less the coupon cost and securities borrowing cost. The same type of report is produced for the long positions. If a trader goes long or short in a sizeable amount for a period longer than a few days it is possible to negotiate a repo with the desk at much finer rates than the typical fixed rates for overnight shorts.

This policy has improved the overall profitability per trade and has considerably increased the awareness among traders of the important settlement aspects of a trade. The 'missing link' has, to an extent, been found, and as more banks start settlement management programmes, the demand for securities borrowing should increase exponentially.

Kassenverein Neu

The major changes occurring in the KV's processing systems as described earlier in this chapter could also further the development of securities lending. Settlement fails should be reduced. With the implementation of matching and same day settlement, it is also expected that the demand to borrow securities in order to cover settlement fails will decrease. The emphasis should shift more towards trading related borrowing. This shift certainly will place more demands on the KV programme for competitive borrowing rates. It will also force more banks to seek new sources of lendable securities, either from end investors or from lending programmes.

There is also debate as to whether or not the KV modernisation will draw more trading counterparties back to the local market for trading and settlement purposes. Clearly one of the goals of KV Neu is to allow the local market settlement mechanism to compete on a similar *niveau* with the offshore settlement systems that have drained settlement business away from the local settlement banks over the years. Some believe that a flow of business will take place back into the market as the barrier of financing costs disappears. Others argue that the business that has left the local market has found more comfortable quarters offshore and will remain there. Another opinion is that the KV Neu is a defensive reaction to protect the business that still remains in the local market before it disappears as well. The end result most probably will be a mixture of all of the above. Some business will flow back to the market but a substantial amount of the offshore business has indeed found a home. At the same time KV Neu should curtail the negative flow of business. The extent that the development of the securities lending business will be affected is clearly dependent on the amount of business that returns to the market. If it is substantial, then one can expect significant growth in securities lending activity. Even a less significant amount will benefit the product.

Attitude of the Local Institutions

The interest of local banks, insurance companies, corporations, and mutual funds in the securities lending and repo products has to be further stimulated to expand the market. The domestic market has to play a larger role in driving the product rather than relegating the responsibility to international lenders and borrowers. As mentioned previously, there has been considerable progress made in generating activity since the KV lending programme was inaugurated, but this is not enough to create more rapid growth. Stronger involvement of local players is a necessity.

SUMMARY

A combination of regulatory changes, deregulation of institutional investors, a plurality of settlement management programmes, improvements in the KV lending system, as well as stronger local market interest, should catalyse the growth of securities lending in Germany. The question is if and when these changes will occur. Certainly significant progress has been made in the market and the future is bright for a fully developed financial vehicle. The relative success of a few active players has been very positive, in effect nudging other players into the market. As the experience level of new entrants increases, the volumes should rise accordingly. The major open question is if securities lending can gain enough momentum to grow into a full-fledged business before declining margins erode player interest in the product. If so, then securities lending in Germany will take its place alongside the leading securities lending markets. If not, its place will be reserved in financial history alongside the many innovative but short-lived products that benefited only a few.

3: The French Market
Michel Sidier, J P Morgan, Paris

In recent years the French market has been one of the fastest growing markets in terms of securities lending.

A bill was formulated in 1987 to relax the tax treatment on stock loans, especially for Capital Gains Tax, and Stamp Duty. A few pioneers started promoting the activity in 1988, and by 1990 it became a 'real' market.

On the bond side, an old technique, the *remere*, used for tax purposes, is now being replaced by a more modern *repo* arrangement called Pension with delivery. However, the French market has developed its own rules and culture. To understand its peculiarities, one has to understand the way the stock market operates, as well as the recent changes which have occurred since 1987, forming part of the French Minibang.

STRUCTURE OF THE SECURITIES INDUSTRY

The Minibang

The law of 22 January 1988 on the French Bourse was the framework which modernised the Paris Bourse, under what has become known as the 'French Minibang'. Although some of these transformations will take some time to implement, these are the main changes which took place:

- The brokers (*agents de change*) became companies with limited liability, instead of partnerships with unlimited liability. Their capital became open to other corporations (generally banks or insurance companies) both French and foreign.
- The quotation by fixing was replaced by a computer-based system where prices move on a real-time basis according to market forces.
- Brokers, banks and some other financial intermediaries may now act as principal.
- A new settlement system at D+3 known as 'Relit' has been installed.

With this new philosophy, the Paris market became similar to the UK or

US markets. It became more open to non-French dealing or non-French participation. It became much more 'international'.

The Various Markets

Paris and the regional Bourses: There are seven French exchanges, Paris, Lille, Lyon, Marseille, Nancy, Bordeaux and Nantes.

They function according to the same rules, and constitute a single market. No arbitrage is possible between the various exchanges, since a stock can only be listed on one exchange.

Paris is, of course, the main centre, and all the blue chip stocks are listed here. However, some valuable stocks of the second market are listed in the regional Bourses.

The Three Boards
The market is organised into three boards, the official market, the second market and the unlisted market:

- The official market lists most of the bonds as well as the largest French and foreign companies. This official market is itself divided into a monthly settlement market for the most active shares, and a cash settlement market for bonds and the less actively traded shares.
- The second market was created more recently. It is aimed at fast-growing, medium-sized companies looking for funds for their expansion. Only 10% of the capital needs to be open to the public.
- The 'over the counter' market is open to any security, without any formality or conditions. It is generally the place for inactively traded securities.

The Monthly Settlement Market
A total of 292 shares are quoted on the monthly settlement market, of which 207 are French and 85 are foreign. This is the blue chip market and follows special rules.

All dealings are by parcels of 5, 10, 25, 50 or 100, depending on the share. The trade can be a multiple of the parcel, but not a part of it. For instance, if one wants to sell 83 Générale Des Eaux for which the trading parcel is 10, he can sell 80 shares on the monthly settlement market, but will have to sell 3 shares on the cash settlement market.

One can sell short, or buy without immediately lodging the cash. There is a margin which is 20 per cent in cash to cover the variation risk (or more if provided in other securities). However, this margin is rarely provided for trades between brokers or banks, either French or foreign.

All trades on the monthly settlement market can be settled on the cash system, but with an increased fee, which make it uneconomical. It also stops most arbitrage temptation.

The general timetable for settlement on this market between Sicovam members is as follows (M being the last working day of the month):

M-5 Liquidation day. It is the last trading day for same month settlement;
M-4 Contango day;
M   Shares and cash settlements.

The contango

On liquidation day it is possible to carry a position, either long or short, through to the next month. This is done the day following liquidation day. Prices for carrying positions are set up on the Stock Exchange through a supply and demand-fixing process. Technically the original trade is settled, a new trade reinstated, and the operator borrows either cash or shares, depending whether he is long or short. The contango (*marché des reports*) is a borrowing technique. We will discuss its advantages and disadvantages later in the chapter.

The Trading

The French brokers still have a monopoly. However, since January 1992 the number of seats allocated to the Exchange is no longer restricted. It is very likely that in the future all European brokers will have direct access to the French market. But for the time being all Stock Exchange transactions involving a French resident must go through a French broker.

Banks can accept orders, but they have to be processed by a broker. In this case the fee is generally shared according to certain rules between the bank and the broker. Banks may also get a share of the fee by acting as agents for the operator (*réponse des ordres*).

The brokerage fee, which used to be fixed, is now negotiable, as in London. This, coupled with the sharp decrease in trading volumes since October 1987, has caused several brokers to lose money. Some are in serious difficulty. It is estimated that, at the end of 1990, 50 per cent of the brokers had problems with an over-capacity of about 30 per cent.

The share prices are established by supply and demand, and managed by computer on a real-time basis.

There are no jobbers, or market makers, obliged to buy or sell at a given price. However, brokers and other authorised financial intermediaries may act as principal within market price ranges (or ±1 per cent if dealing after market close).

Strict rules exist for block trading to ensure protection of the public.
The fixing is still used for warrants, some foreign shares etc.
The timing of the real-time pricing is as follows:

10 am. The opening price is fixed. It takes into account orders already in the system (either unexecuted orders from the day before, or new orders input between 9 am to 10 am).

10 am to 5 pm. The price moves according to market forces. The consequence of the absence of official market makers is that an order is not sure to find a counterparty, even though the price of the order was hit.

5 pm. The closing price is set up.

The Brokers

Originally brokers were appointed by the authorities, and their number was restricted. They were operated as a partnership, and had unlimited liability.

The minibang resulting from the law of January 1988, transferred the broker's personal membership to companies, with limited liability. They became authorised to sell part or all of the shares of these new companies. The *agent de change* (a person) became a company (Société de Bourse).

Most brokers have now become part of a French or foreign group. However, a few are still independent, or share a diversified shareholding.

It was the tradition of the French Bourse to support any broker having financial problems. The other brokers, through a large guarantee fund, would bail out the defaulting *agent de change* and would try to find a successor. In most cases the public would not be aware of anything. The problem was internally managed, and stayed 'in the family'.

Now, due to the change of shareholding, the larger amounts involved (especially in bond trading), and the relative decrease of the guarantee fund, failures are more common, more publicly advertised, and more costly for the public. Beaudoin, Buisson and more recently Tuvier were famous, well established brokers for which the minibang proved fatal.

Regulators
As in most other countries, two main authorities control the Bourse.

The Société des Bourses Françaises is the association of all French brokers. It manages, among other things, the guarantee fund.

The COB (*Commission des Operations de Bourse*) is similar to the SEC, although with probably fewer powers and prerogatives. It controls public information, the efficient functioning of the markets and insider trading situations.

THE SETTLEMENT SYSTEM

All main listed equities and most bonds are kept in a central depository system (Sicovam) under banks' or brokers' accounts. Except for a few registered shares (e.g. Michelin), all these stocks are in bearer form.

Under the old settlement system Sicovam was purely a depository system and did not handle any cash, nor did it undertake to match instructions. However, with Relit now coming into force, there is an automatic matching and a netting of payable or receivable funds.

Types of Stocks

Nearly all stocks on the Paris market are in dematerialised form. However, they can be in bearer form or in registered form:

Bearer Stocks
These stocks are not registered in the name of the shareholder but are held in fungible form on the books of Sicovam, the French depository and transfer agent. All banks and stock brokers have accounts with Sicovam who records the stocks in those accounts.

The account holders are called affiliates and are given an affiliate number (e.g. Banque Indosuez's number is 440). The companies who issue the stocks do not, therefore, know the true beneficiaries.

However, a new category was set up for certain sensitive stocks such as communications stock (the French TV broadcasting TF1 for instance). This is known as identifiable bearer (*Porteur identifiable*), where the company issuing the stocks can ask the banks who the shareholders are.

Most of the stocks on the Paris market are in bearer form. It is worth noting that a bearer stock can be converted at the option of the shareholder, into a registered form (either formal or administered). This is generally the case for institutions or holding companies who want to be seen as a shareholder in a specific company: they will hold their stake in a registered form.

Essentially Registered (essentiellement nominatif)
According to the Articles of Association of certain companies, no bearer shares are issued. Only registered shares are available and these can be in either formal registered form or administered registered form.

The transfer of stocks in registered form normally takes longer than a transfer of stocks in bearer form since the company has to be advised of the change of ownership and the transfer has to be recorded in its books. However, a new procedure installed in 1989 makes it now possible to lend registered stock. The main difficulty is to find lenders of such stock.

A registered stock can be in two forms:

(i) Formal Registered (*nominatif pur*). These stocks are registered directly in the names of the beneficial owners and are recorded and kept by the companies who issue the stocks (or by financial institutions who act as their registrars). Each stockholder is given a unique identification number.

Registered stockholders who hold a minimum number of shares (which varies from company to company) therefore receive from those companies all notifications of annual general meetings, extraordinary general meetings etc., and are advised of all corporate actions.

(ii) Administered Registered (*nominatif administré*). These stocks are registered directly in the names of the beneficial owners in the records of the companies who issue the stocks (or their registrars) but they are not held there. They are held by the financial institutions who act as depositories for the stockholders, and the depositories will, of course, advise their clients of all corporate actions on their holdings.

Sicovam

Sicovam (*Société Interprofessionnelle pour la Conservation des Valeurs Mobilières*) was created in 1949 as a central clearing house with a book entry system (originally voluntary).

In November 1984, all French securities were dematerialised. Any holding of French securities must be by book entry in Sicovam books.

Sicovam now counts:

6,600 securities accepted for deposit, more than 500 members, and 265 sub-members.
535,000 accounts.
80,000 entries per day.
32,000 transfers per day.

Sicovam has been instrumental in designing and implementing the new delivery versus payment system, called Relit. Sicovam has also been given the responsibility of recording stock loans between French residents.

The Settlement System: Receipts and Deliveries Instructions

The Old Settlement System
The old settlement system was a manual system, with a telephone pre-matching. Shares were transferred within Sicovam through a transfer order,

while cash was paid via a Banque de France money transfer. It was not a delivery against payment system, since both cash and shares were exchanged through different systems (Banque de France for cash, Sicovam for securities). This created a delivery risk which the market soon found unsustainable with the increased volumes occurring in the late 1980s.

The development of Relit was seen as an answer to that problem.

Relit

It became evident that the settlement in the Paris market, although in most respects more efficient than the other European markets such as the UK, was far behind the US and the recommendation of the Group of Thirty.

In view of increased competition between various international Bourses, and of greater internationalisation of the markets, the French Bourse devised a five day settlement against payment system known as Relit (**R**èglement **Li**vraison **T**itres).

It is based on a three day (D+3) settlement period. When fully implemented it probably means the end of the monthly settlement period. It also solves one of the main problems of the French settlement system, the lack of a strict settlement against payment system. With Relit the cash and the securities are moved at the same time with no risks for the counterparties.

Unfortunately, the original planning of Relit has been delayed by a year. Relit started in November 1990 on a trial basis, and became fully implemented in 1991. A delivery versus payment takes place as follows:

(i) Receipt of the broker's instructions by the custodian bank.
(ii) Input into the computer system. Among other information, it is required to input a trade date and the exact number of shares. The cut-off time to send instructions is approximately 5 p.m. on the day prior to settlement day.
(iii) Each day a computer listing shows unmatched deals. This allows the two agent banks to liaise and sort out any problems. The deal is re-entered if necessary.
(iv) Each night all trades for the next day value are matched and ready for settlement. Positions are netted off and the balances of securities or cash are credited or debited into Sicovam (for securities) and Banque de France (for cash) between 2 p.m. and 5.30 p.m. on settlement day.
(v) If a trade is not input in time, or if it is rejected, it is still possible to make a free-of-payment delivery with same-day value.

SAME DAY TURNAROUND

Most banks will receive and deliver a stock on the same day. As we all know this is very important for any stock lending activity. However, Relit makes it more difficult than before, when telephone pre-matching used to ensure an on-delivery. Unlike DTC where trades are settled on a real-time basis, Relit settles on a nightly batch, so that all instructions to receive and on-deliver must be in the system the day before.

THE IMPACT OF RELIT ON SECURITIES LENDING

It is generally estimated that Relit will have a very favourable effect on securities lending. Some estimate that the volume of business could grow substantially.

Currently, very little lending business is done for straight settlement. The bottleneck which existed prior to October 1987 has been resolved. Low trade volumes together with massive investments made by the most active custodian banks, has resulted in smooth settlement. The existence of the monthly settlement system, and of the Contango, further enables operators to live without a great deal of stock borrowing.

THE CONSEQUENCES OF RELIT ON THE SETTLEMENT

Like any fully computerised system, Relit makes operations more secure, but less flexible than it used to be.

The two counterparties will input their instructions which need to match exactly. In particular the 'shape' (number of shares) and the trade date will have to be the same.

In a stock loan the trade date has to be the same as the settlement date, to avoid creating dividend and rights problems, since the shares are not sold, but transferred as they are on the settlement day. Some banks did not anticipate the problem and would not accept a trade date equal to the settlement date. In that case the best course of action is to take for trade date, the date just preceding the settlement date. It is thus very important to agree with your borrower or lender all the details (trade date, shape etc.) prior to sending your instructions, in order to avoid any delay. Unlike the old system, your agent bank will not call your counterparty's bank to confirm the settlement. This gives the system less flexibility; but also more security if both trades match perfectly.

Another area of improvement is the money side of settlements. Under the old system we saw that there was a delivery risk. This is now covered by Relit. If your counterparty cannot deliver his part of the deal (stock or cash), the system will stop the delivery of your part.

The three-day settlement system may eventually mean the end of the monthly settlement system. If this is the case it will likely cause the demise of the Contango Market, since it would be too difficult to quote a daily Contango price, or offer it monthly as is done now.

If the volume of trading is large enough, the three-day settlement system should generate a fair amount of settlement-driven stock loans. Short sellers and arbitrageurs who had until the end of the month to net their position and settle, will have no other alternative but to borrow securities under a three-day settlement system.

The only negative effect Relit could have on stock borrowing volumes could be for inter-market arbitrage. When one buys in Paris for example, to sell the same shares in London, taking advantage of two different market perceptions, the settlement problem is aggravated by the different account periods: monthly in France, bi-monthly in the UK.

If all markets trade on a three-day rolling settlement period, then the only problem facing an arbitrageur will be the transfer of shares from one registrar to another. Unfortunately, for the arbitrageur, this is still far from satisfactory.

Dividends and Rights

Straight Dividend
When a company issues a straight dividend, the pay date is the same as the ex-date. The company will pay its paying agent's bank, or Sicovam acting as paying agent, the dividend, as per their position in Sicovam at the close of the preceding day.

The banks in turn will pay their clients as per their position in their books, for the same period. If a bank is not a paying agent, it will have to claim the dividend from a paying agent bank, which takes a few days.

However, the irreversible trend is now for Sicovam to credit the banks directly on dividend day. Consequently, most banks will pay their client with good value.

It is worth noting that, since most shares are in bearer form, the company paying a dividend does not know the shareholders. It only knows, and pays, the banks and brokers who have a Sicovam account.

DRIP

French companies have recently started dividend reinvestment plans (DRIP). The introduction of such plans has modified the old established rule that payment date and ex-date were the same.

In a typical DRIP, a shareholder has about a month after ex-date to decide whether to reinvest the cash dividend in shares or not.

It is important to note that the French DRIP is not a choice between a cash or a share dividend. In all cases it is a cash dividend (with all the tax implications), with an option to re-invest this cash into new shares. This option can be exercised by excess, or by default. When a withholding tax is due, the shareholder must still subscribe for the full amount by topping up in cash the 25 per cent withholding tax.

When the dividend is paid in cash it is generally available at the end of the option period (approximately one week after). When new shares are opted for, they are generally available 3 months after the dividend day.

The option makes stock lending during the dividend period extremely difficult to monitor, and quite hazardous for the borrower.

Any DRIP strategy is made difficult by the existence of a tax credit, called the AVOIR FISCAL.

Avoir Fiscal
A non-resident may borrow from another non-resident over the dividend period. The main problem the counterparties will face is the avoir fiscal.

The avoir fiscal is a tax credit granted by the French Government to induce investors to invest in the share market. Traditionally French investors would invest in gold, bonds, saving accounts and real estate, but would be very reluctant to invest in the share market.

At a time when inflation was running high, and thus dividends were not attractive in comparison to interest rates, the French government agreed to repay to the French investor the amount of corporate tax already paid by the company in relation to the dividend. If the dividend is 10F, the company has paid 50 per cent corporation tax on that amount, i.e. 5F. In addition the investor will pay income tax on the 10F dividend. To make it more attractive to the investor, he can claim back the 5F corporate tax already paid. This is purely a tax credit, with no cash involved. To attract foreigners to invest in the French market, the French authorities decided to grant the same privilege to certain non-residents, but this time payable in cash.

The French apply a withholding tax of 25 per cent to non-residents, but under most double tax treaty agreements, this is subsequently reduced to 15 per cent. On dividend day a non-resident will be paid 75 per cent of the net dividend. If eligible for avoir fiscal, the investor will be able to reclaim an additional 52.7 per cent of the net dividend, the next year, from the French tax authorities. All of his payments would have been 127.5 per cent of the net dividend, which is equal to 85 per cent of the gross dividend (the gross being 150 per cent with the avoir fiscal).

Tax exempt institutions are generally not eligible. But UK pension funds, although tax exempt, are eligible through a January 1988 amendment to the Treaty.

The avoir fiscal can be claimed the year following the dividend payment, as early as January. It is generally paid within six weeks of application.

If a lender is eligible for the avoir fiscal, the choice is to either wait until the following year to be paid, or to demand payment from the borrower immediately. If the lender waits until the following year, there is a risk that the borrower will not be in existence in one year's time. However, if the lender demands the payment immediately, and has the opportunity to invest the proceeds, the borrower is at a disadvantage. A solution would be for the lender to offer the borrower a discount, based on the French Franc interest rate.

WHO CAN LEND AND WHO CAN BORROW: THE LAW OF 1987

Prior to 1987 the French market was not amenable to stock lending. While not strictly forbidden, a turnover tax and a capital gains tax on the disposal of securities made securities lending unattractive. Other techniques existed for bonds, for example the remere (very similar to a repo transaction), and the pension. But none were available for shares.

Under the influence of the professionals in the market, and in view of a greater international opening after 1992, the French authorities passed a bill in 1987, to prevent any penalties in the securities lending market. The bill was revised in 1988.

The main features of the law of 1987 are listed below. While the law is considered very liberal, it is designed to prevent dividend washing, and is monitored closely by Sicovam.

No Lending Over a Dividend Period

A security cannot be lent out over a dividend period. However, there is no restriction on Corporate actions occurring during a loan period.

Bonds may be lent over an interest period if the coupon is *not* subject to withholding tax. Most French government issues are not liable to a withholding tax, and consequently can be lent over the coupon period.

Although this major constraint is due to prevent dividend washing, it also presents some problems for arbitrageurs who may need to borrow stock for a long period of time, i.e., one year or longer. It forces them to borrow the shares offshore (US or UK) where this restriction does not apply.

Duration

The maximum duration of a loan is one year. However, this does not prevent the loan from being immediately 'reinstated'. The main difficulty is, again, the dividend. Shares which do not pay a dividend, such as Eurotunnel, are lendable for a longer period. The only difficulty is finding a lender.

Borrowers

Permitted borrowers: brokers, banks, unit trust funds (up to 10 per cent of their portfolios) etc. Not permitted: individuals.

Lenders

Anyone, including individuals and corporations, may lend their securities. Unit trusts may lend up to 15 per cent of their portfolio, without any specific approval from their unit holders. (They may borrow up to 10 per cent of their assets.)

Insurance companies in France faced specific problems of maintaining technical ratios. A new regulation specific to insurance companies was implemented in June 1989.

Control

All loans must be registered with Sicovam. Some money market instruments must be registered with Banque de France.

Accounting

The law also contains some accounting rules:

(i) All stock lending fees are considered a payment of interest, and thus not liable for VAT.
(ii) The lender uses the LIFO method, while the borrower uses the FIFO method, etc.
(iii) The shares will remain in the lender's portfolio. They will move from the 'investments' account to the 'other loans' account. If any provisions were made for a decline in the share price, those provisions will remain. From an accounting standpoint, the transaction is a loan, even though physically there is a transfer of property.
(iv) For a unit trust, the price of the unit does not change if the shares are on loan.
(v) The borrower must enter the borrowed shares at market price.

The French Market

THE EXISTING LENDING TECHNIQUES ON THE FRENCH MARKET

Contango

On the last day of the current account, operators who have not closed their positions, and who cannot either deliver securities they have sold, or pay for the securities they have bought, may carry their positions over to the next account period through a special market organised each month.

This contango market takes place at D − 4 (D being the last business day of the month). It is only available for shares listed on the monthly settlement market.

The rate at which short sellers can borrow the securities they need until the next settlement day, or buyers can borrow the cash to pay for their securities, is determined by supply and demand. This market operates in the Paris Bourse, with the large institutions acting as natural providers of stocks. Since it is driven by market forces, the cost can vary significantly from one month to another, or from one security to another. The cost of borrowing stock through the contango can vary from as low as 1 per cent p.a. to up to 50 per cent p.a. if the market is very tight.

If stock is borrowed through the contango market over a dividend period, the borrower makes a payment in lieu of dividend at a rate of 100 per cent of the net declared. The major advantage for operators is the ease with which they can access the market. The major drawback is the uncertainty over the cost. For that reason, most market makers and arbitrageurs now tend to access the newly-developed securities lending market.

Remere

In order to develop a repo market, French operators had to overcome two technical difficulties.

- A law of 1964 makes it impossible for any securities transactions (buy or sell) to take place outside the Bourse, where minimum brokerage fees and turnover tax would make any repo totally uneconomical.
- A capital gains tax.

As a way around these difficulties French tax experts found a very old technique, dated 1909, called the Sale with *remere* (*Vente à Remere*). In the daily jargon of the operators, this became known only as *remere*.

The *remere* is a sale with an option for the seller to *cancel* the sale. This cancellation is generally done with an indemnity paid to the buyer, which corresponds precisely to the rebate due on collateral funds (interest less borrowing fees). This rebate is generally based on the T4M (monthly average money market rate) less ⅜ per cent to 1 per cent depending on the market.

The main advantage of the technique is that the original sale is cancelled, thus reversing all tax implications. (However, it is worth noting that this technique cannot be applied for *shares* for which a stamp duty on the contract of a flat 4.80 per cent would apply.)

The main disadvantage is the credit risk taken by the buyer. Since only the seller may cancel the sale, the buyer must rely on the integrity of the seller to complete the arrangement.

Usually the seller would be asked by the buyer to exercise his option to cancel the sale one day after the contract was set up. There is also the risk that the tax authorities may re-categorise the *remere* into a sell and buy-back arrangement. Thus far, no counterparty has ever reneged on its moral obligation to exercise his option to cancel. Any default would drive this party out of the market forever. However, the huge variations of the stock markets since 1987, and a recent problem with a German bank, have alerted the market as to the risk of this technique.

The Stock Exchange *remere*, known as Operation Liee, could be an alternative. It was developed by the Stock Exchange, in reaction to the development of these off-market transactions.

The main difference with the common *remere* is that the transaction is registered through the Stock Exchange at a fee and the repurchase is no longer optional. The reaction of the Stock Exchange was seen as too late and too costly by the market, and in spite of its merit this technique did not really get off the ground.

The *remere* market has declined substantially since the introduction in 1990/1991 of the Pension with Delivery, and only represents about 10 per cent of the repo market in 1992.

Pensions

The Ordinary Pension
The pension is an interbank refinancing technique. Banks with a long position (banks or money market instruments) can finance their position by pledging these instruments to another bank against cash. In most cases the instruments are not delivered, and the financing bank gets a letter from the counterparty stating that these instruments are held to its order.

There is no real legal background for this technique, which has never been really tested. The reason is that it is purely an interbank technique in a country where the authorities would not let a bank go bust.

*The New **Pension Livrée** (Pension with Delivery)*
Both *remere* and the traditional Pensions, present risks for one party to the deal. These risks were ignored in the bullish times. However, following the 1987 crash, the DG bank problem, and the reluctance from foreign operators to enter into *remere* agreements, French operators found it necessary to develop a new technique.

Banque de France was very familiar with the Pension, which was being widely used on the inter-bank market. It was therefore very natural for the Banque de France to propose a new Pension agreement to the market, with the support of the tax authorities (Ministry of Finance).

Although the technique of Pension was already in use before, the new agreement brings several major enhancements.

(i) The old Pension was not governed by any law, regulation, or contract. It was purely a market practice. The new Pension is governed by a market convention, and will probably be ratified into law.
(ii) The old Pension was specifically an inter-bank arrangement. The new Pension will apply to all counterparties.
(iii) The old Pension was generally without delivery. The borrower of cash would segregate eligible paper to the lender of cash. This was possible when dealing took place within the group of the major French banks, upon which strict monitoring and control was imposed. Under the new system all Pensions will be against delivery.
(iv) The pledge of securities is very formal in France, and the previous system had never been tested in court. There were questions about the tightness of the collateral. The new system should give better protection in case of default.
(v) Although accepted as a market practice, the traditional Pensions did carry a fiscal risk. The new system received an agreement from the Ministry of Finance exempting it from any tax side-effects, i.e. capital gains tax, stamp duty etc. (letter from the Finance Minister of December 1990).

The new Pension with delivery is very similar to a repo, in which there is a sell and a buy back at a definite price, for a definite period.

While less flexible than a loan, the new Pension could represent a major advantage if it is possible to carry a deal over the dividend day. However, there is still some uncertainty as to how this will be treated.

Securities Lending

The contango is used solely for shares, while the ordinary pension and the *remere* are used solely for bonds or other debt instruments. The peculiarity of the securities lending technique (as well as of the new *Pension Livrée*) is that it can be used for both shares and debt instruments.

Organised through the law of 1987, and revised in 1988, stock lending started out with a great deal of scepticism. However, it has grown in acceptance since then.

The main advantage of this technique is that its rules are clearly defined by the 1987 law. The main disadvantage is that a French resident may not cross a dividend period in a lending transaction.

The cost of borrowing varies from 1.5 per cent to 3.5 per cent, depending on market forces, and on the number of intermediaries involved in the trade.

On the domestic side, the technique poses some conflict with the Banking Act if cash collateral is involved. Non-financial institutions are not allowed to accept cash deposits, and the payment of interest on cash deposits is strictly limited to banks and a few other registered financial institutions. The solution has been to subscribe to short-term money market funds, and lodge the units as collateral.

The other problem is the relative complexity of pledging assets under French law. It is generally a very formal and costly procedure, not compatible with the variations in loan value which rule this business. Furthermore, in the case of a company defaulting and applying for the French equivalent of Chapter 11, the Administrators could have a good case to consider the collateral as non-pledged and the lender as an unsecured creditor.

However, a recent amendment dated July 1991 makes it possible for the collateral to be transferred outright to the lender in case of the borrower's default. The pledge is thus replaced by a reciprocal obligation to repay the loan against the return of the collateral. The same would apply to the lent securities in case of default of the lender.

THE SECURITIES LENDING MARKET

Most banks, institutions, unit trust and treasury departments of large corporations are involved in the *Remere* or pension market, which is estimated at FF50 billions.

The stock loan market is much more restricted in its number of players.

The Lenders

- Unit Trust Funds.
- Insurance companies and pension funds: however, insurance companies only started lending following the implementation of the statutory order of June 1989.

- Brokers: only a couple of brokers became active as lenders. Cheuvreux de Virieu (Group Suez) and Schelcher Prince became very active in this market as intermediaries.
- The banks: Banque Indosuez has been the first and the most active player in this market since its beginning. However, most banks now offer such a program: Société Générale, CCF, Banque Paribas, J.P. Morgan, etc.

  Indosuez and more recently Paribas also have a desk in London. It is worth noting that BNP, which is not very active in France, opened a desk in London in 1991; it closed in 1992.
- Other institutions. Some government agencies, with large portfolios, have been quite aggressive in lending out their securities. Some industrial companies have also taken advantage of the product.

The Borrowers

French and foreign brokers are the main borrowers. Derivative funds are expected to become more involved. In 1990 huge amounts of shares representing the CAC40 were borrowed by arbitrageurs. In 1991 the arbitrage was reversed and brokers started lending their long positions at very fine spreads.

The Intermediaries

The main intermediaries are Banque Indosuez, Cheuvreux de Virieu and BBL Intermediation. More recently Société Générale and J.P. Morgan joined the party.

Sicovam acts as a registration office, as per the 1987 law, but gave up its initial idea to provide for automatic loans.

It is worth noting an interesting initiative, called 'cotinter'. 'Cotinter' was formed as a Club deal by Compagnie Parisienne de Reescompte and Société Générale. It grouped the major French banks in an effort to better match supply and demand. Securities for loans, and securities to be borrowed were entered into a computer. The cotinter system would then allocate offered securities to operators looking for them. A certain lack of flexibility in the system, and the fact that the business cannot be reduced merely to computer input has prevented this idea from being successful. Cotinter shut their doors in November 1991.

A Few Practical Rules

Before borrowing French securities, one has to be careful of a few rules.

Callable: a French resident cannot lend any shares over the dividend period. When borrowing French shares, make sure you know if the lender is resident or non-resident, since that will make the securities callable or non-callable.

Avoir Fiscal: if the lender is non-resident, he is likely to claim the 50 per cent avoir fiscal. This has to be taken into account in any arbitrage deal.

Fixed versus open-ended loans: due to the monthly settlement system and to the obligation to indicate a term to Sicovam for each loan, most lenders will automatically assume you take the securities for one month. If you want the ability to repay earlier, this has to be negotiated separately and confirmed in writing. By the same token, if you want to avoid being recalled at the end of the month, you have to indicate to your lender that you wish to automatically renew the loan until further notice.

Cancellation: the market in France operates on a strict observance of the oral commitment. If you take shares, you cannot easily unwind the borrowing. In most cases you will have to pay 1 month's fee, even if you called back 5 minutes later to cancel.

Settlement: the settlement is generally efficient, and same day turnaround is possible with most agent banks. However, the new computer system, Relit, is somehow less flexible than the old manual procedure. Make sure your counterparty indicates the same trade date, shape and consideration if you do not want your settlement to be delayed.

Fees: Fees are generally computed on 100 per cent of the market value instead of 105 per cent. Except for repos, French lenders or borrowers are not familiar with the rebate system. They will pay or receive interest on their collateral, at the daily market rate (TMP), and pay or receive a stock loan fee at month end.

CONCLUSION

The French market wants to become one of the leading European markets. In recent years many innovations have shown the willingness of the authorities to support this objective. Paris is a major futures and options market through the MATIF. Settlements are efficient through a dematerialised system, and moving towards a three-day settlement procedure called Relit. French authorities have also encouraged the development of securities lending, both on *bonds* (*Pension Livrée*) and shares (stock lending). With its numerous warrants, convertible bonds, options and its various rights issues, not to mention its foreign shares traded on the monthly settlement market, Paris is a market offering a great variety of arbitrage opportunities. In the past few years we have also tried to make it easy for people to lend and borrow, to make these arbitrages as smooth as possible.

4: Lending Securities in Japan
Jiro Takahashi, Mitsubishi Finance International, London and Makoto Yokota, Sumitomo Trust, Tokyo

HISTORY OF THE JAPAN SECURITIES FINANCE CO., LTD

The Japan Securities Finance Co. was founded in 1950 as an institution specialising in securities finance. It was licensed in 1956 as a securities finance company according to the Securities and Exchange Law. It then began lending operations directed at securities companies, individuals and corporations with emphasis on loan transactions.

In 1971, legislation was enacted regarding foreign securities companies, which prompted the development of the stock loan market in Japan. In response to this, the Japan Securities Finance Co. began general stock loan operations in 1977 distinct from its other loan transactions.

Operations presently conducted by the Japan Securities Finance Co. include:

- Margin transactions
- Bond loans directed at securities companies
- General loans to securities companies
- Security loans for individuals and corporations
- Operations as a payer of original interest on government bonds and general stock loan operations

Margin transactions are loan transactions where the stocks lent to selling customers are borrowed from the Japan Securities Finance Co. by a securities company. In margin transactions, individual investors provide a set amount of margin money to borrow the purchase amount and stocks from the securities company for trade activity.

When stocks are required for settlement of accounts in the trading activities of securities companies, the Japan Securities Finance Co. often provides those stocks. These are general stock loan operations of the Japan Securities Finance Co. and the target of such general stock loans are limited to securities companies. When a security company is unable to settle its trade accounts, the due-bill system is used on the Tokyo Stock Exchange. This requires cash collateral. Yearly interest is very high at 14–15 per cent, so that excessive use of due-bills is not advisable.

Japan's account settlement system is stricter than those abroad, since companies are required to settle accounts within a period of four business days.

The Japan Securities Finance Company's prices were formerly linked to the long-term prime rate. However, due to requests from foreign securities companies, this is currently set at a lower rate. Nevertheless, foreign securities companies, due to mutual trading with life and non-life insurance firms as well as banks, have gained opportunities to obtain stocks at lower rates.

In the market incident known as Black Monday, a large volume of sales from abroad resulted in a shortage of stocks. Since then, the Japan Securities Finance Co. has taken a positive stance toward increasing the number of sources from which stocks can be obtained. The Japan Securities Finance Co. is further attempting to diversify the key procurement sources in stock loan operations while increasing their coverage and offering stock loan services at lower rates to meet the needs of customers.

DOMESTIC LENDING

Definition

'Domestic lending' is first defined in terms of the character of the lender and borrower as seen from the standpoint of the Foreign Exchange and Foreign Trade Control Law. There are the following possible trading patterns:

Pattern	Lender	Borrower
Case 1	Resident according to Foreign Exchange Law	Resident according to Foreign Exchange Law
Case 2	Non-resident according to Foreign Exchange Law	Resident according to Foreign Exchange Law
Case 3	Resident according to Foreign Exchange Law	Non-resident according to Foreign Exchange Law
Case 4	Non-resident according to Foreign Exchange Law	Non-resident according to Foreign Exchange Law

Case 1 is defined here as 'domestic lending'. This 'domestic lending' includes the following cases:

(a) Margin transaction and loan transaction operations as the business of the Japan Securities Finance Co.
(b) General stock loan operations as the business of the Japan Securities Co.
(c) Mutual loan transaction between an institutional investor (lender) in Japan and a securities company (borrower) in Japan.

Margin transactions are aimed at both corporations and large individual investors, although there are relatively few corporations involved. (As in trading by individual investors, the ratio for margin transaction remains at about 40 per cent.)

Restrictions concerning such trades are based on the Securities and Exchange Law, the individual regulations of the Stock Exchange and restrictions concerning loan transactions. The original purpose of the margin transaction system was to maintain fair price formation through fluidity of the stock market by the introduction of theoretical supply and demand.

The loanable stock names that are the targets of loan transactions are section one of the first division names on the market. Depending on the method of borrowing, the outcome will vary.

For this reason, the second class of general stock loan operations was created. However, the loan rate is generally lower for these loan transactions. In contrast to (b), the mutual loan transactions described in class (c) involve companies.

Thus, depending on the supply–demand situation for stocks, the borrowing rate can fluctuate, as is the case on the New York and London markets.

The Development of the Tokyo Market

Development of domestic lending business
Starting around 1985, representatives of major securities firms in Europe and the US began visiting the Tokyo Market. They carried out feasibility studies on the possibility of mutual trading between lenders and borrowers without the intercession of the Japan Securities Finance Co. Efforts were made to open the market in conjunction with advisory authorities and institutional investors. It has been said of the Tokyo Market that it tends to resist change. It was certainly extremely difficult for representatives of European and American securities firms to overcome this resistance. The underlying problem was that relatively few of Japan's financial institutions, and significantly, only a very few employees of Japan's leading securities companies, had a clear understanding of the meaning of the English term 'securities borrowing and lending operations', or understood the differences between transaction, loan transaction and general stock loan operations at the Japan Securities

Finance Co. The very idea of stock loans was totally foreign and new to them. Now, seven years later, the concept of 'securities borrowing and lending operations' is quite generally understood.

Trade Practices on the Tokyo Market

Major borrowers
Japan's major borrowers are members of the Tokyo Stock Exchange who utilise the Japan Securities Finance Co. as their primary source for stock lending.

In the case of mutual trading, close relationships have been formed with many institutional traders in the forty years since the end of World War II.

For subsidiaries of foreign securities houses who are members of the Tokyo Stock Exchange, the primary lender of Japanese equities is the Japan Securities Finance Co. (Non-members act through members in transactions carried out by the Japan Securities Finance Co., Ltd.)

Borrowing is limited for margin transactions due to restrictions regarding the purpose of borrowing, as well as the limited supply of loanable stocks. It is necessary therefore, for the foreign securities houses to go to the general stock loan services of the Japan Securities Finance Co. or to trade direct with institutional investors. The next step is to search for institutional investors who would become lenders.

Market practices – The system of sharing stocks ('mochiai') among financial institutions and corporations
Since the start of the Meiji Era (1868), Japanese industry has had its foundation in the state. This resulted in the emergence of *zaibatsu* (powerful Japanese conglomerates officially dismantled in 1947. An informal structure, however, still exists today). Procurement of funds was handled by the banks belonging to the individual *zaibatsu* and stocks were issued using a method of sharing stocks (*mochiai*) among the industries and banks belonging to the *zaibatsu*. These practices have continued to this day. Corporations and banks have developed inseparable relations among parties who consider themselves 'in the same situation'. Stock investment by lending institutions include both 'political investment' and 'pure investment'. 'Pure investment' is normal stock investment established for the purpose of pursuing capital gain and is most suited to stock loan engagements. 'Political investment' refers to the above-mentioned *mochiai* stocks. These form the overwhelming majority of stock investments and, as a result, discourage fluidity of stocks.

Stocks Held by Life Companies

Portfolios held by life insurance companies are amongst the largest in the world. However, a large part of these are political investment stocks and there are cases where the agreement of the issuing body is required when handling stocks loan. While the leading life insurance companies have been lending stocks both to the Japan Securities Finance Co. and to Japanese securities companies for quite some time now, the actual sums involved are not significant.

The limit for loans is generally 55 per cent of a company's total assets. This includes the amount of the loan.

The types of shares differ depending on whether the life insurance companies are part of *zaibatsu* or are independent. This is an important point to remember when considering life insurance companies as lenders.

There are, however, some life insurance companies who will not lend securities due to company policy.

Stocks held by non-life insurance companies:

Compared to life insurance companies, the amount of stocks held is much smaller and only the major non-life insurance companies have the leeway to lend stocks. As for the engagements of non-life insurance companies, almost all of these are policy investment stocks. Thus, in the case of actual lending, there are cases where the permission of the issuing company is required. The restriction on the total framework for loan stocks is 55 per cent of total assets. However this includes the internal limit of 30 per cent of the lending amount (based on 'Manual for Use of Assets').

An increasing number of non-life insurance companies are also starting to engage in stock loan operations in order to increase the dividend rate for cumulative insurance.

Stocks held by city banks, regional banks and long-term credit banks:

Japanese business features a 'main bank' system for dealings with their trading partners so that the balance of stocks held is strictly controlled. As a result, it is considered very serious when the share of stocks held in a particular industry fluctuates at the end of a business period.

These held stocks are known as 'political investment' stocks. Although this situation is unthinkable for overseas investment institutions, it is the norm here.

Moreover, at certain banks the name of the shareholder is included on the back of the shares. Of prime importance is that the name of the main bank be included on the first line in the upper left on the back side of the shares. If these shares were to become the target of stock lending, it would mean that the 'virginity' of the main bank had been violated and this would not be permitted out of concerns for the loyalty of the bank toward the customer.

If this virginity were to be violated so that shares with the bank's name were circulating the market in large volumes, there are concerns that the policies of the main bank toward the issuing company would undergo changes.

For this reason, the shares that become the target of stock lending at the banks are sometimes political investment engagements, where there is no fear of the above problem, and pure investment engagements that have been established simply for the purpose of obtaining capital gain. However, this is a very small amount compared to the balance of shares held by the bank.

Stocks held by trust banks

The life insurance companies and trust banks are the major suppliers of lendable securities. These include assets held as pure investment, political investment, annuities, *tokkin* and fund trusts, although it is mainly the first three that become the targets of stock loans. They are particularly large suppliers to the Japan Securities Finance Co.

Restrictions on stock lending

As a general rule, there is no stock lending in political investment shares when shares reach a record date.

In cases where changes (increase in capital, dividends, etc.) are expected due to questions of rights, it is required that the title to the shares be returned by the record day. In other words, there is no lending of shares over the record day.

Delivery/transfer difficulties

The custody transfer system on the Tokyo market is still under development and transfer operations are therefore done manually. The transport costs, insurance and labour costs that accompany this are considerable. As a result, there is a tendency towards avoiding inefficient stock loan trading. Lenders are not enthusiastic about small lots (units of a thousand shares) or cases where the loan period is only for a week or less.

The Tokyo Market, Present Situation and Demand for Borrowing Stocks

The present state of the Tokyo Market

The sudden increase in general stock loan operations has originated from the sale of large volumes of Japanese stocks by foreign institutional investors following Black Monday in October 1987. Since then, there has been a major shortage generated at the foreign securities companies and custodian banks.

Since mid-1988 there has been an increase in the issuance of foreign bonds by Japanese companies, especially convertible bonds (CBs) and bonds with warrants. When these share prices are rising, there is lively hedge-selling and arbitrage. This in turn necessitates spot stocks and there is an increase in stock loan operations.

In addition, since 1989 there has been lively arbitrage trading with the Osaka Stock Exchange 50 Futures and Simex Nikkei Average Futures as well as spot and futures trading with Topix. Currently, there is also block trading. For European and American securities companies attempting to develop this type of business in the Tokyo market it was necessary to obtain Japanese stocks in the greatest possible volumes and covering the greatest number of names. In addition, it was the responsibility of the lender to carry out this process quickly and at the lowest cost.

Some of the major foreign securities companies were successful in locating lenders of Japanese equities at 'reasonable' cost.

Market Practices or Domestic Lending

This section will deal with the trading forms and business procedures of the life and non-life insurance companies who are the main providers of portfolios.

Participants in the lending market:

- life insurance companies.
- non-life insurance companies
- securities firms
- foreign securities firms

Types of stock held: Life and non-life insurance companies belonging to *zaibatsu* have a tendency to hold many shares in companies belonging to the *zaibatsu* companies. Stocks are held in even distribution. This is a major point to remember for foreign securities companies looking for lenders.

Size of the loan stocks: The ideal size of a stock loan from a lender's perspective is 500,000 shares of a single name.

Lending period: One week to three months is the average term of a stock loan.

Lending rate: The long-term prime lending rate is the benchmark rate. Variations are possible based on loan size and lending period.

The rate is often calculated based on how many *sen* per day. As a general rule this includes interest both for the day the loan is taken out and for the day of repayment, on a 365-day basis.

Extension of lending period: possible.

Partial repayment of loan stocks: possible.

Collateral: Letters of credit issued by Japanese banks are the primary form of collateral. Japanese Government Bonds, Negotiable CDs (stocks) may also be used as collateral.

Miscellaneous: The shares of life and non-life insurance companies are held in common with the other issuing companies. Thus, when lending stocks it is necessary to have the permission of the issuing company.

Qualifications of partners in trade: Many life and non-life insurance companies demand of the borrower that the person responsible for business negotiations be able to speak Japanese.

Required documents and related matters:

A written contract regarding lending of securities
A Letter of Guarantee from the bank

Written applications for borrowing securities, one for the time of application and one for the time of borrowing. At return of shares, a certificate is also issued.

Communications procedures: Almost all communication between borrower and lender is done by facsimile or telephone.

Procedure of delivering securities: A company employee on the borrower side, or a member of the representative company, is responsible for physically delivering the equity securities.

INTERNATIONAL LENDING

The Definition of International Lending

Pattern	Lender	Borrower
Case 1	Resident according to Foreign Exchange	Resident according to Foreign Exchange
Case 2	Non-resident according to Foreign Exchange	Resident according to Foreign Exchange
Case 3	Resident according to Foreign Exchange	Non-resident according to Foreign Exchange
Case 4	Non-resident according to Foreign Exchange	Non-resident according to Foreign Exchange

Cases 2 to 4 in the above chart are defined as International Lending.

Currently, trading as defined in Case 2 is still rare compared with the others. Thus, this section will deal only with Case 3 and Case 4.

Non-resident lender
Non-resident lenders are the various institutional investors who have relatively large quantities of Japanese stocks. The master custodians holding these stocks lend them in order to increase the value of their custody services and to increase their own profits.

Resident lender
The Foreign Exchange and Foreign Trade Control Act has led to differences of opinion between the resident as lender and the non-resident as borrower.

The Foreign Exchange and Foreign Trade Control Act is not applicable in loan transactions (*chintaishaku-torihiki*) between residents and non-residents. It only applies in consumer loan transactions (*shohitaishaku-torihiki*). There are differences between loan transactions (*chintaishaku-torihiki*) and consumer loan transactions (*shohitaishaku-torihiki*). In the case of loan transactions (*chintaishaku-torihiki*), there is a duty to return exactly the securities that one has borrowed. In the case of stocks, for example, one must return the stocks with the same serial numbers. In the case of consumer loan transactions (*shohitaishaku-torihiki*) it is sufficient to return securities of the same type and amount as those borrowed. One should also remember that there are differences between loan transactions (*chintaishaku-torihiki*) and consumer loan transactions (*shohitaishaku-torihiki*) regarding their treatment under Japanese tax statutes.

Consumer loan transactions (*shohitaishaku-torihiki*) of securities from a resident to a non-resident would involve a combination of two types of trading: (i) The non-resident obtains securities from a resident (at time of implementing stock loan), (ii) A resident obtains securities from a non-resident (at time of returning loan stocks). When the securities that are the object of trade are Japanese stocks, then regarding section (i), there is a duty to make a formal notice to the borrower according to the Foreign Exchange and Foreign Trade Control Act. However, when one party in the exchange is a designated securities company or when the trade takes place via a designated securities company, the borrower does not require submission of notice.

In the case of collateral by deposit of cash, permission is required under the Foreign Exchange and Foreign Trade Control Act. However, if a bank authorised for foreign exchange is handling this for its own account as lenders, permission is not required. Also, if collateral is not in the form of cash but rather L/Cs, securities or the like, this is not subject to permission or submission of notice according to the Foreign Exchange and Foreign Trade Control Act.

Life and non-life insurance companies have started lending on a limited basis to foreign securities companies with offices in Japan.

Long-term credit banks and city banks do not yet have a firm policy for the following reasons: (i) All banks take a very cautious stance toward lending proprietary stocks and particularly stocks held as part of company policy because they want to maintain a good relationship with their customers; (ii) There are administration problems with custody accounts received from non-residents. In general, banks are more conscious of organisational finance than the insurance companies and are currently experimenting with lending out a section of their own stock.

In general, trust banks take the same stance as the long-term credit banks and city banks. However, in addition to stock lending, some trust banks are able to lend from trust accounts, a facility that is unavailable to the long-term credit banks and city banks.

A balance between organisational finance and resistance here to increased operational costs and overseas trading, needs to be achieved. The growth of the market is being fuelled by the demand of the non-resident borrower.

Practices for International Lending

Trading practices for international lending of Japanese stocks have been based on existing practices of major US and European securities firms. However, local laws and customs must be taken into consideration.

Contracts
A comprehensive securities lending agreement is drawn up between a borrower and lender. These contracts address the respective rights and duties of the contracting parties.

The form of transactions
Generally, all loan transactions are treated as consumer loan contracts in which the ownership rights to the loaned securities are transferred to the borrower. From the standpoint of the lender, this transaction is not a trade with conditions attached to repurchasing the securities. Instead, it is a clear case of lending, and must not become the object of securities exchange taxes or taxes on capital gain.

Lending and borrowing period
Most stock loan transactions are 'open ended'. This means there is no fixed term for the loan. The contract continues unless there is special notice from the lender or the borrower. However, the lender and borrower determine between themselves whether the securities to be lent out are 'callable shares'

that are principally returned prior to the record day of the issuing company or 'non-callable' shares that do not definitely have to be returned prior to record day.

Settlement period
Generally, two days after the trade day or any day thereafter can be the settlement day. In some cases, however, there is so-called 'quick start' in which delivery takes place the day after the trade is done.

Returns and recalls
Generally, returns may be called in to the lender for next day settlement. When there is a recall from the lender, the settlement day is usually five business days after filing of the request. In addition, when the borrower receives a request for return from the lender, he either obtains this security from another lender and returns them or he uses other means such as a purchase on the market. This period of five business days has been decided on in view of the time difference with Tokyo, plus the four business days required for purchase on the market. Also permitted is partial repayment in which there is partial return of the shares that were originally lent out.

Many Japanese lenders recall their stocks prior to record dates in March and September.

Collateral
Collateral can take the form of cash, letters of credit and letters of guarantee. In addition, both the borrower and lender mark to the market with the closing price each day and thus check whether the collateral is at an appropriate level.

CASH COLLATERAL
Normally, cash collateral is placed in a lender's account designated by the lender. One day prior to the anticipated settlement day in Tokyo, the borrower deposits an amount in the lender's account that is equal to at least 105 per cent of the current market value of the securities. Securities are marked-to-market daily. If the market value of the loaned securities rises, the borrower will be asked to pledge additional collateral to bring the total collateralisation up to 105 per cent. If the market value of the loaned securities falls, the borrower may request back some collateral to bring the total collateral back up to 105 per cent.

LETTERS OF CREDIT AND LETTERS OF GUARANTEE
Letters of credit or letters of guarantee may also be used as collateral. In these cases, the lender must not only investigate the creditworthiness of the borrower but also the creditworthiness of the issuing bank.

Lending Securities in Japan

Procedures are similar to those for cash collateral since there must be daily checks on the current market value of the securities lent and the maximum guarantee amount. When the current market value of the loaned securities in question (or 105 per cent of the market value) exceeds the amount of the guarantee agreed on by the lender and borrower, steps must be taken to increase the maximum guarantee amount or add new letters of credit or letters of guarantee.

Borrowing and Lending Fees

CASH REBATES

A rebate is utilised when the borrower pledges cash collateral to the lender. In this instance, the lender invests the cash collateral in the market-place, earning interest. The lender then rebates back to the borrower a portion of the interest earned. This rebate is always negotiated in advance between the borrower and the lender, and rarely changes during the life of the loan unless there are major changes in market rates and interest.

FEE METHOD

The fee method is employed at times when there is non-cash collateral. In this case, the fee is multiplied by the market value of the loan, and multiplied by the number of days outstanding (360 or 365).

OTHER ISSUES

Stock loans are generally collateralised at 105 per cent of the current market value of the underlying stocks. In loans denominated in US dollars, rebates and fees are calculated on a 360-day basis. For those loans denominated in any currency other than US dollars, a 365-day year is used.

Lending and Borrowing Beyond the Record Date (Kigoshi)

This refers to lending and borrowing securities the term of which crosses over the record day or interim record day of the company issuing the applicable loan securities. During this period, because there is an extreme shortage of lenders, lending and borrowing fees increase. Also, the so-called non-callable shares for which lending and borrowing beyond the record day is possible, generally have a higher fee than callable shares.

When stock loan transactions cross a record date the borrower must make the lender 'whole', as if he had never lent the stock. This is true regardless of whether the dividend is a 'cash' or 'stock' dividend.

In addition, due to the so-called '5% Rule of Large Holding' that was implemented in December 1990, the collateral agreements and other contracts used in loan stock transactions are considered important contracts.

The lender who is defined as a large holder has an obligation to report it to the Ministry of Finance and file copies of that report to the issuing company and Stock Exchange.

TAXES

From the standpoint of the lender, when carrying out lending and borrowing beyond the record day (*kigoshi*), an amount equal to the benefits (such as dividends) generated by the loan securities is collected from the borrower. However, as was mentioned previously, international lending itself is formed by consumer loaned contracts (*shohitaishaku-keiyaku*), which mean the ownership rights of the loan securities are transferred to the borrower. Thus, many lenders take a negative stance toward trading beyond the record date due to the tax problems involved. For example, if the benefits are a dividend and there is trading beyond the record date, the lender posts the cash amount equal to the dividend received from the borrower as part of the charge for lending of goods. This cannot be booked as a dividend and therefore cannot be treated as profit in relation to the dividend received. Moreover, it can no longer be the subject of tax credit and thus loses any tax benefits. Generally speaking, this tax reduction effect is judged to be greater than the profit for lending shares beyond the record date.

THE PRESENT SITUATION FOR INTERNATIONAL LENDING

Cost of borrowing/lending

Although domestic lending uses the long-term pure rate in Japan as a benchmark, the lending fee for international shares is about 2 per cent. Compared with the figure of 25 to 35 basis points, which is the general level for US stocks, this is still an attractive market for lenders.

From the standpoint of the resident as lender, the fee for lending shares at 2 per cent for international lending is perceived as low, yet many people are attracted by the size of the international lending market. Additionally, the increase in business opportunities will probably encourage increased participation in that market. However, when those responsible for lending US stocks engage in loan operations with Japanese stocks, they may feel that the lending fee of 2 per cent is rather high. This demonstrates the gap which continues to exist between domestic lending and international lending.

Physical limitations in the Tokyo Market

The Tokyo market is still carrying out most of its settlements by hand-delivery of certificates. Therefore, there are operational costs for both the lender and the borrower. However JASDAC started bank-transfer operations in October 1991. This will eventually lead to great efficiencies in the settlements of securities. There are also limitations on settlement deadlines. This is particularly difficult when there is a same day borrow and loan.

Problems resulting from the relative newness of the International Lending Market

Although trading practices are based on mutual trading between non-residents, there are several problems that still have to be ironed out for resident lenders. They include the inconsistency in computing the lending fees, inconsistency in contracts, the lack of a common system and linkage between the general system and the domestic system. Owing to the immaturity of this market, there are likely to be many potential lenders who are not yet participating.

THE OUTLOOK FOR DOMESTIC AND INTERNATIONAL LENDING OF JAPANESE STOCKS

The international lending market in Tokyo is still immature. It is important to note that there are considerable differences between the practices for domestic lending on the Tokyo market and international lending overseas. Up until this point the non-resident borrower has been in the position of promoting development of the market. We expect to see increased influence in this market from the resident lenders such as the trust banks, life and non-life insurance companies, long-term credit banks and city banks. Hopefully, domestic lending and international lending will start to get in step with each other in terms of lending practices and borrowing costs.

5: Financing Transactions as Short-term Investments
Steven R. Meier, Merrill Lynch, New York

Thus far, we have focused on international securities lending on a country-by-country basis, or from a micro perspective. Included in our discussions have been various issues which affect our businesses across the board. Information involving settlement procedures, transactions costs, tax, legal and regulatory concerns, implications of cross-currency, cross-border and cross-cultural trading and the problem of dealing in several time zones affect all of us regardless of venue. The very specific information included throughout this text will prove invaluable as your trading operation springboards you into the global market for fixed income and equity securities lending and position financing.

While one cannot effectively argue that distinct information regarding the characteristics and nuances of a particular market is without importance, it is critical that we also have an appreciation for the 'Big Picture'. Just as it is common for students of economics to first study microeconomics before moving to macroeconomics, I believe it is beneficial to first understand the workings of the individual repo markets which comprise the world-wide repo market. Indeed, an appreciation of basic units is required if an understanding of the broad system is to be garnered.

Although we have examined several of the most active world repo markets in the earlier portion of this text, we have yet to analyse the workings of the most developed repo market in the world, that of the United States. Since this market is the final 'basic unit' which must be analysed prior to a view of the 'Big Picture', we will begin with an in-depth look at the workings of such. Included herein will be a detailed analysis of the past problems occurring in this market. Hopefully an enriched comprehension of the world-wide risks of our market can be acquired through reading this chapter.

Following our analysis of the US market, we will begin our study of the macro system with a brief look at the world economy as a competitive market for global capital and resources. This will be followed by a discussion of the essence of a 'financing transaction', the need to borrow relatively lower cost money. We will then look at the basic forms of secured borrowing in the international markets. Next, we will examine a recent international repo market situation, which shall serve as a warning to investors who are not properly protecting their investments through prudent business practices. This will be followed by a brief list of suggested guidelines for transacting such business.

INTRODUCTION TO THE UNITED STATES MARKET FOR REPURCHASE AGREEMENTS

Repurchase agreements, commonly referred to as repos, are money market transactions in which one party sells securities to another while agreeing to repurchase those securities at a forward date. These transactions possess several characteristics associated with a secured loan, with the lender of money receiving securities as collateral to protect him against borrower default. In fact, repos are hybrid transactions and are frequently viewed as securities sales with subsequent purchases by some market participants and secured loans by others. Thus, one should be aware that parties putting up money are referred to as either 'investors' or 'lenders', while parties putting up securities are referred to as either 'sellers' or 'borrowers'. The terms 'securities' and 'collateral' are also interchangeable. These distinctions will become clear once we have discussed the hybrid nature of repos in greater detail.

The American market for repo transactions has experienced dramatic growth both in US dollar terms and range of products during the past decade. This has been the result of an explosive growth in US government debt, new and aggressive cash management procedures brought about by the high interest rate environment of the late 1970s, and an enhanced use of arbitrage and other sophisticated investment strategies that employ repos. In May 1987, US government primary dealers alone were borrowing, on an average daily basis, $290 billion in the repo market and lending $273 billion in the reverse market.

The terms 'repurchase agreement', 'repo', 'RP', and 'reverse repo' are all used to describe the same transaction. One firm's repo is another firm's reverse repo; both are the same transaction viewed from two different perspectives. It is common street practice to view the transaction from the dealer's perspective. A dealer looking to borrow money is transacting a repo, while a dealer looking to borrow securities is transacting a reverse repo. For example, when a customer delivers money to a dealer, the transaction is often termed a repo by both parties.

- One firm's repo is another firm's reverse repo.
- Dealer borrowing money is transacting repos.

- Dealer obtaining securities is transacting reverse repos.

Today, the repo market enjoys a favourable record characterised by safety, efficiency, competitiveness, and innovation. However, this market has had its share of problems in the past which resulted in financial loss to a number of institutional investors. Past problems were rare exceptions, and have been addressed by US regulatory authorities to ensure that this vital part of the nation's financial markets continues to flourish and perform its very necessary functions. The following is detailed informational writing designed to educate and enlighten readers on the key aspects of the repo market in the United States.

THE MECHANICS OF REPOS

As indicated above, a repo is the sale of securities on a temporary basis, involving the seller's agreement to repurchase the same or similar securities at a later date. The other party has a corresponding obligation to sell them back. The repurchase price may include an interest component, or the sale and repurchase prices may be the same with interest paid separately for the use of funds. In the United States repo market, the party lending money (the more liquid asset) usually receives 'margin' to provide a safeguard against market fluctuation and potential risk of default. To provide this margin, securities used as collateral are often priced at market value minus a 'haircut'. The size of the haircut varies depending on the maturity, price volatility, scarcity and current market price of the underlying collateral, as well as the term of the repo and the credit standing of the lender. Interest is paid based on the actual number of days using a 360 day year. Most repo transactions are carried out for cash settlement (same day settlement), unless both parties agree otherwise. The following example illustrates these concepts.

Example: Suppose that Merrill Lynch has $1 million worth of US Treasury Notes trading at par and needs to finance them overnight. Suppose also that an investor such as a corporation, bank trust department or a local government has $980,000 in cash to invest for one day. In this instance, the two parties can enter into an overnight repo transaction.

Merrill Lynch agrees to deliver the $1 million worth of US Treasury Notes to the investor (lender) and receive $980,000 in funds. Here, Merrill is giving the lender a 2 per cent margin, by taking a 2 point haircut off the current market price (assume zero accrued interest). The repo proceeds would be:

$$\text{\$ Amt of repo} = (\text{price} - \text{haircut}) \times \text{face value} + \text{accrued interest}$$
$$= (1.00 - 0.02) \times \$1 \text{ million} + 0 = \$980\,000$$

The $1 million in US Treasury Notes is to be returned the next morning by the lender to Merrill Lynch. Merrill simultaneously wires funds to the lender for $980 000 plus interest on one day's use of the funds. Assuming a 7 per cent overnight repo rate, the lender will receive interest in the following amount:

Interest paid to lender = $980,000 × 0.07 × $\frac{1}{360}$ = $191.

This is a repo transaction in its simplest form.

REPO COLLATERAL

The most active forms of securities in the US domestic repo market are government treasury and agency issues, mortgage-backed pass-through securities, and money market instruments. Repos involving asset-backed securities, whole loans, and corporate bonds are becoming increasingly common. In the rapidly developing international repo market, the most common forms of collateral include foreign sovereign governments, supranationals, and eurobonds. In the US repo market, the market value of these securities should always exceed the repo dollars invested when used as repo collateral. This is due to the margin given, as described earlier. Margin should be maintained to best protect the lender from loss should the market value of his collateral fall below the dollar value of the repo transaction. This is accomplished by 'marking-to-market' collateral to reflect price movements in the value of underlying securities. If the market value of the collateral falls, and the margin is not maintained, the borrower of money must give the lender either additional collateral or cash to meet the margin. Currency fluctuations will also affect the percentage of collateral where cross-currency transactions are involved.

It is important to note that throughout the repo transaction, the borrower of money remains the beneficial owner of the collateral even though he temporarily places the collateral in the lender's possession. Accordingly, the borrower retains the right to all coupon interest accruing on the collateral. Coupon payments are also passed through to the borrower when paid.

Also worth noting is the distinction between 'general' or 'stock' collateral and 'special issue' collateral. This distinction most often arises when the dealer is seeking to obtain securities, via a reverse repo. General collateral is collateral which meets the dealer's general requirements, while special issue collateral describes the situation where the dealer is looking for a specific security. For example, a dealer reversing in general treasury collateral will accept any bills, bonds or notes, while a dealer looking for special issue collateral will only accept that issue, such as the current treasury long bond.

This collateral distinction will be further addressed in our discussion on reverse rates and dealer matched book operations.

TYPES OF REPOS

There are basically four types of repo transactions. They are as follows:

1. *Overnight repo.* The most common of the repo types is the overnight repo. Approximately 80 per cent of all repo transactions are done on an overnight basis. These transactions terminate the next business day (so trades done on Friday to come off the following Monday are still considered overnight repos).
2. *Term repo.* Repos transacted for durations exceeding one business day for a specified dollar amount and with a fixed termination date are called term repos. Term repos can have a maturity as short as two days and as long as a year. Subject to negotiation, investors in term repos may liquidate at market levels, as with any other money market instrument.
3. *Open repo.* Transactions in which a dealer and lender enter into an agreement whereby the lender agrees to give the dealer repo money for an indefinite term are called open repos. This arrangement may be terminated by either party at any time, and the collateral may be substituted daily, while the lender has the right to adjust the repo dollar amount. The dealer may change the interest rate daily to reflect current market conditions. Here, the dealer is given an unconditional right of substitution with regard to collateral.
4. *Flex repo.* Here, the lender agrees to give the dealer money at a specified rate with a stated end date providing, however, that the lender may withdraw some of the cash loaned before the expiration date based on a prearranged drawdown schedule. Thus, the lender locks-in the term rate while maintaining some degree of liquidity.

DELIVERY OF REPO COLLATERAL

Most repo transactions are executed on a 'delivery versus payment' (DVP) basis whereby the lender actually takes possession of the collateral in some manner (note that this method of settlement is similar to the delivery against cash – receipt against payment, or DAC-RAP, common in the international markets). This is the safest way to execute a repo, since the lender has secured a 'perfected' lien on the collateral. However, not all repo trades involve actual delivery of collateral. Both situations will be discussed here.

When repo trades are executed between dealers or with depository institutions, collateral is received into their bank clearing accounts or general accounts. This is a simple procedure which is performed with both physical and wireable forms of repo collateral. For lenders of money who do not have established clearing accounts and are not depository institutions, receipt of repo collateral is possible through both a tri-party relationship with the dealer, its clearing bank and the lender, or an investor's custody account at a bank. Both are discussed below.

Tri-party repos are transactions in which the dealer and the lender enter into a repo and have the trade cleared through a third party bank, which is usually the dealer's clearing bank. The bank is involved in both sides of the trade, taking in money from the lender and crediting the dealer's cash account while simultaneously moving the collateral to the lender's custody account. Here, the collateral is actually being moved from the dealer's clearing account to the lender's custodian account. This method of delivery is cheaper for the dealer because it does not incur the cost of delivering the collateral outside the bank. On termination date, the bank will not release the repo collateral back to the dealer until it receives the lender's money. Tri-party repos require a signed agreement between the three parties involved in the trade. Part of this agreement provides for establishing the lender's custody account at the dealer's clearing bank as well as providing for the rights and responsibilities of all parties under a tripartite arrangement. Note that tri-party delivery cuts down on fails because one bank reconciles both sides of the transaction.

Most repo transactions are executed on a DVP (DAC-RAP) basis whereby collateral is delivered to the lender's custodian bank. This method of taking possession is similar to tri-party repos, with the main differences being that the dealer does not necessarily use the third party bank as its clearing agent, and no tri-party agreement has been entered into. Note that these transactions are more expensive for the dealer who incurs the cost of delivering collateral to a bank other than its clearing bank.

Repos in which the dealer does not actually deliver collateral to the lender but rather segregates collateral at either (a) its clearing bank or account at a central depository and designates it as collateral for a specific customer, or (b) maintains the collateral on its premises, are called 'hold-in-custody' repos. They are also referred to as 'letter repos'. The collateral is moved from the dealer's clearing account to a special account for the exclusive benefit of repo customers. This is a cheaper way of transacting repo for the dealer since clearance fees are not incurred. A strong incentive for the dealer to use 'hold-in-custody' repos exists when the collateral being pledged is either cumbersome or expensive to deliver. 'Hold-in-custody' repos are most often preferred when the collateral includes physical securities, money market paper and wireable odd-lot positions.

From a safety standpoint, 'hold-in-custody' repos are the most risky form of repo for lenders. It is important to realise that 'hold-in-custody' repos are not necessarily unsafe transactions, but the safety factor is impacted by the creditworthiness of the dealer.

DETERMINATION OF REPO AND REVERSE REPO RATES

A number of factors influence repo rates. In the market for overnight repos, these factors include a benchmark money market rate such as Libor or the Federal Funds rate, the general supplies of repo money and repo collateral, the quality of collateral, the delivery mechanism, the size of the transaction, and the credit worthiness of the dealer. These supply and demand forces and qualitative factors also apply to dealers and markets outside the United States. The lender will receive a rate which reflects the riskiness of the transaction and current liquidity within the system relative to the demand for money. The most visible reflection of the overnight market for money in the US market is the Federal Funds rate, which is the rate at which banks borrow and lend their excess reserves. Repo rates will move in general concert with the Fed Funds rate daily. Thus, the lender of money receives a rate which reflects both the riskiness of the transaction and the cost of settlement to the dealer, as well as the overall market condition prevailing when the trade is negotiated. Repo rates are not established by a set formula or a standard spread to Federal Funds or Libor. Rate relationships are dynamic and may change daily as market conditions require. An additional point worth noting is that repos are secured arrangements, while Fed Funds and other interbank transactions are not. Thus, high quality repo often trades at some spread below Fed Funds. (Note that it has been uncharacteristically common for US Treasury repo to trade *above* Federal Funds during the early 1990s. This has been attributed to a real or perceived 'credit crunch' in the marketplace.) This is also true because many investors, including dealers, municipalities and corporations do not have access to the Fed Funds market.

In the market for term repo, factors affecting repo rates include those mentioned above along with the shape of the short-term yield curve, the right to substitute collateral, yields on competing money market instruments, seasonal influences and interest rate forecasts. All these factors are considered when establishing rates.

As we have discussed the factors affecting repo rates from the dealer's perspective, we will now look at some factors affecting reverse repo rates (when the dealer is seeking collateral). Remember that a dealer may be looking for either 'general' collateral, that collateral which meets his general requirements, or 'special issue' collateral, a specific security issue.

In theory, general collateral reverse levels will be about the same rate at which similar term repos are being done. However, dealers will actively pursue a positive spread on such positions by charging a higher interest rate on their money to borrowers through reverse repos than they are paying out to their lenders doing repos. Thus, it should be a surprise to no one that reverse rates quoted by a dealer will be higher than their offered repo rate. The spread between the two rates reflects the spread the dealer is earning on this matched trade.

Special issue collateral will trade at whatever rate the market will bear at a given point in time. Dealers seeking special issues are most often doing so to cover a short position, which occurs when the dealer sells a position he does not own, and needs to make delivery of this issue before the price drops and he buys it back. The rate at which a dealer can reverse in the issue will depend on the availability of the security on the street and the demand for the specific issue. Accordingly, if the entire dealer community is short a specific issue and needs to cover its shorts, and demand for the issue clearly exceeds supply, the rates the dealers will charge reverse customers may be several hundred basis points below the reverse rates for general collateral. This is still cheaper for the dealer than an outright fail to deliver.

THE MATCHED BOOK

A repo trader at a dealer firm is responsible for financing his firm's trading inventory of securities along with trading what is referred to as a 'matched book'. Dealers engage in trading a matched book for profit, which consists of reversing in securities (dealer lending money) and repoing the same securities out (dealer borrowing money) for a spread. In the simplest terms, the repo trader is buying and selling money through a series of secured transactions for a spread. He attempts to earn a higher rate of interest on the money he lends versus the rate he pays for funds borrowed.

For example, the dealer may lend money to a thrift through a reverse repo at 7 per cent and receive GNMA securities as collateral, then borrow money from a lender through a repo paying him 6¾ per cent and give him these same GNMA securities as collateral. Here, the dealer is earning 7 per cent on his money while he pays his lender 6¾ per cent on the funds he borrows, creating a 25 basis point spread to the dealer. The dealer will attempt to 'match' the end date of the repo with the end date of the reverse. If successful, the repo and reverse come off on the same day, so he can receive in collateral from the lender and return it to the thrift. This is where we derive the term 'matched book'. If the dealer does not match the end date of the repo with that of the reverse, he will be 'mismatched', and have a 'tail' to the trade. Tails represent interest rate risk for the matched book trader. If the repo comes off before the reverse, the dealer may be required to pay another investor a higher rate of interest on a new repo if rates have risen. This may result in a negative carry on the tail of the trade, i.e., repo rate higher than reverse rate. However, if rates have fallen, the dealer can pay the new lender a lower repo rate, earning a higher spread on the tail. Repo traders will purposely mismatch their book in this fashion if they anticipate lower interest rates in the near future.

Occasionally, the dealer will enter into a repo which has a longer term than the reverse repo. This can only be done if the dealer retains at least one right to substitute collateral, which would be negotiated when the repo is initially transacted. Here, the dealer must do an additional reverse to obtain replacement collateral for his repo customers. If interest rates move higher, the dealer will be lending out his money to another thrift through a reverse repo at, for example, 7¼ per cent, while he continues to pay his lender a repo rate of 6¾ per cent. The dealer now earns 50 basis points on this portion of the trade. Alternatively, if interest rates should fall, the dealer may be lending his money through a reverse to another thrift at, for example, 6¾ per cent, which puts him in a breakeven situation for this portion of the trade. Repo traders will purposely structure their mis-matches in this manner if they expect interest rates to increase.

Often, a dealer will be mis-matched for a short period of time, because once the reverse is transacted it may take a few days to find a lender to do the repo side of the trade. He will finance these positions on an overnight basis until the other leg of the trade is found and the spread locked-in.

Besides being an excellent source of low risk profit, matched book trading activities provide the dealer firm with several additional benefits. By offering customers financing through reverse repos, the dealer's trading desks enjoy an increase in overall trading activity. This 'one stop shopping' concept makes selling trading ideas easier for account executives when they offer clients long position financing, short position coverage and related futures markets trades. These transactions are integral parts of 'basis trading' and other sophisticated trading strategies. The matched book operation also enhances firm trading efficiency by providing a source of securities to cover trading fails to deliver. In addition, matched book repo traders provide the firm's trading desks with a rich source of market information concerning short-term interest rates, overall short positions held by dealers on the street, short positions held in specific issues, the general liquidity of investors and Central Bank activity.

DEALER'S AVAILABILITY OF REPO COLLATERAL

As stated, the dealer's repo trader finances the firm's trading inventory while also trading a matched book. His collateral positions, and consequently his needs to borrow money, change not only day-to-day, but also intra-day.

For example, if the dealer's government trading desk feels that interest rates will fall in the near future, the desk wants to be 'long securities' to benefit from future price appreciation. This will increase the need for repo financing. Alternatively, if the desk feels rates will rise, it will attempt to hold a very small inventory of securities to protect against the impending decline in bond prices. He may also 'short the market', selling securities he does not own. Shorts may also be undertaken to facilitate a customer's demand for securities, even though the dealer has a 'flat' inventory in the issue. This will decrease the repo trader's need to do repos, and possibly increase his need to do special issue reverses to cover these short positions.

Like the bond trader, the repo trader also wants to be long collateral if rates decline. He accomplishes this by doing reverse repos, and financing the position on an overnight basis until rates fall in an attempt to capture a larger spread (mis-matches his position). This increases his overnight repo needs as he must finance his matched book inventory daily until he puts it out on repo for term. Alternatively, like the bond trader, the repo trader wants a very small matched book inventory (unmatched position) if interest rates are rising to protect himself against having to pay higher rates to his repo customers than he is earning on his outstanding reverses yet to be matched. The repo trader may also short the market by doing repos with a right of substitution for terms longer than his reverses. This way, when the reverse rolls off, he may enter another reverse transaction earning a higher rate on his money if rates have risen, and pair this off against the outstanding repo by giving the repo customer this replacement collateral. Again, this locks-in a higher spread on the tail portion of the trade.

On an intra-day basis, the firm's inventory position and 'unmatched' matched book position changes while trades are done for cash settlement. On the government trading desk, for example, a trader may buy or sell treasury securities for cash (same day settlement), moving the amount of financing required up or down. Also, the repo trader may put on a new term reverse for cash settlement, increasing his need for overnight financing until he can do the matching side of the trade, the term repo. Note that both the treasury bond trader and the repo trader may also negotiate cash (same day settlement) sales of their inventories, thereby decreasing the overnight need for financing.

Although the need for overnight repo money changes constantly, some dealers will accommodate their repo customers when they do not have enough collateral to satisfy these everyday lenders. The repo trader does this by reversing in collateral on an overnight basis, and uses this collateral to do additional repos with his customers. By facilitating lenders in this manner, the repo trader ensures himself a constant universe of overnight repo customers. This benefits the dealer, because by fostering long-term working relationships with its sources of funding, he will not have to pay-up substantially when overnight financing needs swell.

PARTIES INVOLVED IN THE REPO MARKET

In addition to securities dealers, the major participants in the US repo market include bank trust departments, municipalities, corporations, financial institutions, insurance companies, mutual funds and money market funds. These entities use repos as a flexible, low-risk, short-term investment vehicle.

State and local governments are heavy users of the repo market. The recent reductions in federal support of many state and local projects within the United States have encouraged more aggressive cash management. In addition, repos are adaptable to the uneven seasonal cash flows experienced by many municipalities, counties, school districts, and states. The ability to tailor the maturity of repos and amounts invested day to day makes them especially well suited for entities experiencing unpredictable cash flows. Most importantly, repos are very safe transactions if proper procedures are employed to safeguard the lender.

The Federal Reserve is also a major user of repurchase agreements in the US market. The Fed uses repo as a vehicle through its open market committee to either temporarily drain or inject reserves into the banking system (most central banks engage in similar activities). The Federal Open Market Committee (FOMC) is authorised by the Federal Reserve Act to buy and sell securities and to lend against collateral at the discount window. The Act does not authorise the Fed to make collateralised loans or borrow on a collateralised basis either from banks or non-bank dealers. Therefore, in order to make temporary adjustments in bank reserves, it uses repos and what is called 'matched-sale-purchases' (MSP); the latter transaction resembles a reverse repo from the dealer's perspective and is commonly referred to as 'matched sales'. The Fed initiates overnight or short-term MSP to drain the system, while it initiates 'customer repo' and 'system repo' when injecting Reserves (note that 'customer repo' is done with foreign central banks having US dollars to invest, while system repo involves transactions with bank and non-bank entities which are members of the Fedwire 'system').

A variety of institutions use reverse repos to liquefy securities portfolios, and to take advantage of arbitrage opportunities by providing a source of cash for investment into higher yielding instruments. This works to enhance the overall yield of the investment portfolio.

REPURCHASE AGREEMENTS: A HYBRID TRANSACTION

As described earlier, US style repo transactions possess characteristics of both secured loans and securities transactions. Some of the more important factors relating to both are mentioned here.

Financing Transactions as Short-term Investments

1. Factors supporting the view that repo is a secured loan:
   - accrued interest on collateral belongs to the borrower of money.
   - interest and principal payments pass-through to the borrower of money.
   - margin is given to the lender of money.
   - securities are commonly 'marked-to-market' to maintain margins.
   - borrower of money may retain a right to substitute collateral.
   - sale and repurchase price may be the same, with interest paid separately.
   - securities used as collateral are priced with a haircut.
2. Factors supporting the view that repo is a securities transaction:
   - repurchase agreement contracts are written to indicate a securities transaction.
   - market participants frequently do reverse repos to obtain control over securities.
   - the Fed accounts for matched sale-purchases as securities trades.
   - market participants include institutions who are unable to do secured lendings.

THE EVOLUTION OF THE REPO MARKET

The repo market was little noticed until the spring of 1982, when a few under-capitalised government bond dealers with repos outstanding experienced severe financial distress. The major problems occurred primarily at two dealer firms, Drysdale Securities Corporation and Lombard-Wall, Inc. New procedures were implemented to safeguard repo investors in reaction to these problems. This seemed to calm the repo market until two dealer firms, ESM Securities and Bevill, Bresler and Schulman, failed in 1985, causing substantial customer loss. Three of these failures will be examined here. Past problems of the repo market have all been addressed by regulatory authorities, restoring safety and confidence to this vital market.

Drysdale Government Securities, Inc. (May 1982)

Drysdale Government Securities built a massive government trading position with minimal capital. The firm is estimated to have amassed long and short positions amounting to a few billion dollars, with a very limited capital base. Drysdale's practice involved entering into reverse repos through an agent to obtain high coupon securities nearing a coupon date. Drysdale put up cash close to the dollar price at which these securities were trading ('flat pricing', i.e., without accrued interest), then sold the bonds in the open market for the current trading price *which included accrued interest*. The accrued interest was quite substantial on high coupon issues and provided Drysdale with significantly more cash than it was paying out on its reverse repos. Drysdale was then using this cash to speculate in the market. When coupon interest payments are paid, the holder of securities on reverse passes the coupon payment through to its counter party in accordance with standard street practice. When a coupon payment for $160 million came due, Drysdale could not meet its obligation, which created panic in the government bond market.

Drysdale had done most of its reverse business through a major securities lending bank. When Drysdale defaulted, the Bank asserted that it was merely acting as agent, not principal, and therefore could not be forced to meet Drysdale's coupon payment obligations. Eventually the Bank agreed to take responsibility for Drysdale's positions assumed through transactions with the bank.

In reaction to Drysdale, the New York Federal Reserve Bank ordered all recognised primary dealers to include accrued interest in pricing securities used as collateral in repo and reverse repo transactions. The street now employs 'full-accrual pricing' on all such transactions.

Lombard-Wall (August 1982)

Lombard-Wall (LW) had entered into a series of 'flex repos' which, as described earlier, enable a lender to lock-in a term interest rate while maintaining the ability to decrease the dollar amount of the repo. LW was executing these repos with several municipal entities who would float a bond issue for a construction project that required cash payouts over several years. The municipality would then invest the bond proceeds over the estimated life of the construction project in flex repos, giving them the ability to decrease the dollar amount invested based on a drawdown schedule.

A safe way for a dealer to be able to quote a fixed rate on flex repos is to purchase securities with maturities spread over the life of the repo, and pledge these securities as collateral for the repo. Apparently LW chose to quote term repo rates and invest the Funds short term, expecting to invest in higher yielding longer-term instruments once rates had risen in accordance with their interest rate forecast. This strategy would have enabled LW to earn a larger spread for the term of the flex repo if interest rates had in fact increased. However, when rates declined, LW was forced to invest in lower yielding instruments, and was left paying a higher rate on its repos than it was earning on its investments. This resulted in large losses for Lombard. When Lombard defaulted, a major investor was left with a sizeable under collateralised repo. Lombard had not given the client possession of the collateral it purchased for them, but rather provided a safekeeping receipt, which it was unable to back with securities having a market value equal to the amount of the receipt.

Term and open repos and reverse repos typically include the right for both parties to reprice collateral to reflect current market conditions, called 'marking-to-market'. Margin calls should be required by both parties if the collateral is above or below a given margin percentage or moves a predetermined dollar amount. This is a common street practice.

Lombard-Wall forced regulators and the courts to address the question whether a repo is a secured borrowing or a purchase and sale of securities. The US Bankruptcy court in New York ruled that repos were in fact secured borrowings, which meant parties holding securities as collateral against a repo could *not* immediately liquidate because the automatic stay provisions of the 1978 Bankruptcy Code became applicable. This created an outcry on Wall Street, which along with support from the Federal Reserve, caused the Bankruptcy Code to be amended in 1984 through an Act of Congress to allow the immediate liquidation of underlying repo collateral (discussed below).

In an attempt to cure the LW case problem, Wall Street began drafting repo agreements which used language reflecting a securities transaction and not a secured loan. With the passage of the Bankruptcy Amendment of 1984, the issue of purchase and sale versus secured loan became moot. Passage of the Amendment also led to the drafting of a standard repo agreement, which the US government dealer community and Public Securities Association (PSA) endorsed. This agreement is now the Street standard.

The Bankruptcy Amendment (July 1984)

The Bankruptcy Amendments exempt certain repurchase and reverse repurchase agreements from an otherwise automatic stay (freeze) on a bankrupt party's assets. Under this law, underlying collateral in a repo or reverse repo agreement is no longer frozen and may be liquidated directly by the repo participant (the entity that has an outstanding repo or reverse repo agreement with the bankrupt party). This ability to liquidate the underlying collateral in a timely and effective manner greatly lessened the perceived risk in repo transactions which prevailed in the repo market after the Lombard-Wall case in late 1982. The collateral must of course be in the possession and control of the liquidating party.

It should be noted that the amendments exempt repo and reverse repo agreements only where underlying collateral consists of either certificates of deposit, eligible bankers' acceptances, or securities that are obligations of, or that are fully guaranteed as to principal and interest by the United States government or agencies thereof. The amendments apply only to repo or reverse repo with a maturity of one year or less. The amendments do not define repo or reverse repo agreements as the purchase and sale of securities or as a loan but as a simultaneous transfer of cash versus a simultaneous transfer of securities. Although these amendments were a welcome clarification for the financial markets, they did not relieve investors of the responsibility to see that the appropriate margining of collateral and the possession of the collateral is secured.

The liquidation provisions are applicable only to those situations where a petition in bankruptcy has been filed. In addition, the new amendment applies only to those institutions coming under Chapter 11. Prior to actual bankruptcy, however, contractual provisions for default would ordinarily permit liquidation.

ESM Government Securities, Inc. (March 1985)

ESM Government Securities, Inc. was a small government securities dealer located in Fort Lauderdale, Florida. When the firm collapsed in 1985, investors, many of whom were small municipalities, experienced losses totalling over $300 million. In addition, 71 state-insured thrift institutions located in Ohio were temporarily closed to avert a depositor run as a direct result of ESM's failure.

ESM was involved in transacting repos (borrowing money) with municipal investors and reverse repos (lending money and obtaining collateral) with thrift institutions. ESM focused on entering into repos with highly rate-sensitive municipal investors who did not take possession of repo collateral. ESM would offer these lenders a higher yield on their money if the trades were done on a 'hold-in-custody' basis. This firm would send each repo customer a letter stating that securities had been placed in safekeeping accounts at its clearing agent. However, ESM was pledging the same identical collateral to several lenders at the same time. By double and triple pledging collateral, the firm was able to take in more cash than it needed to finance its securities position. When the situation became public, many customers were left undercollateralised and without possession of collateral. The effects of ESM rippled out to its customers, resulting in many municipal lenders being placed on Standard and Poor's credit watch 'with negative implications' because the ability of lenders to access collateral was in question.

One of ESM's larger reverse repo customers was a state bank located in Ohio. This bank had pledged over $600 million in securities as collateral for loans (reverse repo) with ESM. When it became clear that this state-insured thrift had not received adequate cash versus the securities pledged, and stood to lose a significant sum of money, its depositors moved quickly to withdraw funds. This prompted the authorities to impose temporary limits on withdrawals from certain banks in the State until the situation could be brought under control.

While some of the problems associated with ESM may have involved fraudulent activities, customers could have avoided or greatly limited losses by following certain procedures and prudent management practices. By properly evaluating the counterparty to the trade, including their corporate structure and capital strength, taking control of collateral and maintaining proper margin, the risks involved in these transactions could have been greatly reduced.

The Government Securities Act of 1986

In reaction to the ESM and Bevill, Bresler and Schulman dealer failures, the United States Congress passed the Government Securities Act of 1986. This legislative Act addressed several problems associated with the 'unregulated' government securities dealer market, and provided regulatory oversight of all dealers in this market. Dealers that had not previously been regulated by the Fed or other appropriate regulatory agency are now required to be registered with the National Association of Securities Dealers (NASD). The Act also put forth a series of rules designed to regulate certain practices of the market-place. These rules relate to the capital adequacy of dealers, custody and use of customer securities, the mechanics of repo transactions, financial reporting and recordkeeping.

US Government securities dealers today must meet minimum net capital requirements, established through an exacting accounting formula. 'Hold-in-custody' repo collateral held at a bank must be maintained in a segregated account 'for the exclusive benefit of repo customers'. In addition, all dealers are now required to have annual outside audits of their financial statements conducted. With specific regard to repos, net capital charges have been structured in a manner which encourages dealers to price collateral properly, and to mark-to-market collateral when market price fluctuations dictate. Any participant who engages in 'hold-in-custody' repo must enter into a written repo contract with specific disclosures on risk contained therein.

The US repo market today is a market characterised by safety, efficiency, competitiveness and innovation. The problems of the past have been addressed by regulatory authorities to ensure market safety. It is important that all repo market participants have some knowledge of its history and the measures that have been taken to ensure that repurchase agreements remain flexible, low risk, high yielding money market instruments. An informed customer base is an essential element of a safe and efficient market.

FINANCING TRANSACTIONS AND THE 'BIG PICTURE'

In this section, we will examine the motivations of dealer financing activities and its impact on the 'Big Picture'. Here, we are exclusively looking at the market for general collateral or, more precisely, that collateral which satisfies the general requirements of a cash lender to secure a loan.

At first glance, the role of 'position financing' appears minuscule when looking at the global market for capital. This initial impression is likely to stay with the less sophisticated observer who assumes that the real action is in stocks and bonds. However, the astute individual will quickly realise that the essence of finance trading is leverage and money, which is the life's blood of the capital markets.

As discussed earlier in this chapter, dealers run highly leveraged operations. From a comparatively small equity base, dealers are able to take large positions in securities as part of their market making activities. This is accomplished through borrowing money via unsecured and secured arrangements. Issuing commercial and corporate bonds, as well as tapping certain types of bank lines, are examples of how dealers leverage themselves on an unsecured basis. Repurchase agreements, which are secured financings, are often at times the major source of financing (i.e., the largest liability) of a securities dealer. It is logical to ask the question, 'Why go through the trouble of providing collateral under a repurchase agreement when I can borrow on an unsecured basis?' The reason for doing so is quite simple; borrowing money against collateral is generally a cheaper source of financing for many dealers than borrowing unsecured. This should surprise no one given the leverage of the average dealer.

It is worth mentioning here that while repo matched book activities range in the tens of billions of US dollars for several large broker/dealers in the US markets, their international matched book activities are rather small in comparison. One factor contributing to this anomaly is the lack of a liquid market for general collateral outside the US. The inability of dealers to take down issues for term periods on speculation of a rising demand for these securities and financing them for short periods at reasonable rates renders mismatched positions a poor use of the firm's resources. However, as European holders of cash become aware and comfortable with secured lending through 'repurchase agreements' they will begin to use repos as short-term investments instead of leaving money on deposit at a large universal bank. Thus, time and energy allocated toward educating holders on the attributes of fully-collateralised investments is well spent given the importance of this source of funding to the dealer.

Lower cost sources of financing help contribute to the profitability of dealing firms. While this is only one of a multitude of factors which impact dealer performance, it is indeed a critical element. As dealers generate profits through their market making activities, other entities are enticed into the market-place, thereby increasing competition and eventually lowering the cost of funding for various entities and companies worldwide. In addition, such activities directly contribute to a better allocation of global resources as world capital markets become more efficient.

While it is naive for one to believe that the world market for capital revolves around general collateral financing transactions, it is also naive to assume that such activities do not affect the demand for capital. It is essential to comprehend the importance of the financing function to profit seeking entities guided by the free hand of competition in the market-place and the impact, however minor, of such activities on the efficiency of the world economy. Bearing this in mind, dealers have a keen interest in ensuring that such sources of low cost financing are protected and remain viable. Thus, self policing of the market-place is essential, since any mishap in the market for repos which financially hurts cash lenders will indeed negatively impact the dealer community.

INTERNATIONAL FINANCING TRANSACTIONS

At the outset of the analysis of the US repo market I stated, 'One firm's repo is another firm's reverse repo.' While this is still generally true, the statement requires a footnote when dealing in international repos. That footnote should read, 'One firm's repo may actually be another firm's sale and buyback.' Here, we begin distinguishing a US style repurchase agreement from a Sale/Buyback transaction.

As discussed, US style repos are hybrid transactions possessing characteristics of a securities transaction and a secured loan. US market conventions and bodies of property and commercial law provide the framework through which this trading arrangement developed. However, the elements which contributed to the formation of this transaction are specific to American markets. In the international markets today, these hybrid transactions appear with increasing frequency as US houses and non-US dealers familiar with the history of the US repo market advocate its use. The concepts of excess margin and marking-to-market of collateral seem prudent and serve to entice cash lenders into trading due to the safety of the arrangement.

Notwithstanding the use of this hybrid transaction within the European markets, confusion often arises due to different conceptions as to what constitutes repo. What is commonly referred to as a 'repo' in many European markets is considered a sale and buyback transaction in the US. While still a financing transaction involving a forward obligation to 'repurchase' securities, sale/buybacks differ in the following ways:

- transactions are actually two separate securities trades *without* characteristics that point to a secured loan
- both trades are executed at the same time, i.e., spot and forward using an investment rate to derive the forward contract price
- excess margin is generally not provided by cash borrower (i.e., flat pricing at 100 per cent market value)
- the lender of cash receives title to the securities while also becoming the outright owner of such (thus, the concept of beneficial ownership retained by the dealer does not apply)
- collateral is not usually marked-to-market
- generally the borrower of cash does not have a right to substitute collateral
- sale and repurchase prices differ. Sale price is the market price, and the repurchase price is the original market price plus or minus the difference between the bond's coupon rate and the agreed upon financing rate
- master repurchase agreements are generally not executed
- accrued interest and coupon belong to the lender of cash (i.e., holder of title)

As we can see, this transaction has characteristics which are quite different than US style repos. Here is an example of a sale/buyback trade (remember we view this trade from the dealer's perspective):

Merrill Lynch (dealer) needs to borrow DMs to finance a DM 30MM German bund position for one month. Merrill offers to a German corporation holding excess cash DM 30MM of 1 May 2001 bunds beginning 2 August 1991 and ending 2 September 1991. In return for the cash loan, Merrill will pay an 8.80 per cent interest rate annualised based on a 360 day year. Therefore:

1. Merrill sells to the lender bunds at a price of 97.94 plus accrued interest on 2 August versus payment of DM 29,877,520.83.
2. Merrill buys back bunds from lender at 97.99676 plus accrued interest on 2 September versus payment of DM 30,103,926.05.
3. In sum, the lender received DM 226,405.21 on its loan of DM 29,877,520.83 for 31 days at 8.80 per cent. In this example, interest income can be derived by subtracting the spot price from the forward price, or calculating the amount of interest earned on 29,877,520.83 at a rate of 8.80 per cent for 31 days based on a 360 day year.

While a sale/buyback transaction is not foreign to the US markets, such arrangements comprise a very small percentage of total financing trades. Some American investors are unable to participate in US style repurchase agreements. This may be due to regulatory restrictions, individual corporate bylaws forbidding such activities, having an accounting system better suited to booking spot/forward trades, or the inability to administer marks-to-markets and/or substitutions of collateral. Since our business is customer driven, most dealers will accommodate these transactions.

While US style repurchase agreements and sale/buybacks ('European Repos') are distinct arrangements with pros and cons associated with each, they are both common in the international markets. Despite their differences, however, both forms of trade have a similar economic benefit for the lender of cash. Interest rates achievable in both transaction types hover slightly below (5-15 bps) currency LIBOR rates. As with the US market, however, interest rates on 'repos' backed by international securities are not determined by an established formula, but are rather functions of supply, demand and risk. Both trades deserve close consideration by holders of short-term cash positions due to their degree of flexibility and relatively high rates of interest given the risks of a fully secured investment. At the end of this chapter is a list of guidelines for investing in such arrangements.

XYZ BANK – FEBRUARY 1990

As discussed thus far, the US market for repurchase agreements experienced some distress in the early 1980s. This was primarily due to a period of rapid growth coupled with a poor regulatory structure to police market participants and practices. In this regard, we will continue with a brief analysis of a relatively recent situation which sent shudders through the growing international market for repurchase agreements.

The purpose of this section is to educate market participants of possible pitfalls in the repo market. Therefore, specific details of the parties involved in this situation are not required to achieve our objective. In addition, the situation to be discussed is rather complicated and, at the time of this writing, has not been settled by the German courts. Since the situation arose from the questionable trading practices of a few individuals, it would be unfair to risk tarnishing the reputation of a large, well regarded German bank. Therefore, the institution in question will be referred to as XYZ Bank for the purpose of our analysis.

XYZ Bank is a German banking institution. In February of 1990 it was discovered that XYZ was embroiled in a bond trading scheme involving several billion German Marks of mostly German sovereign debt. The dispute specifically involved XYZ's obligation to repurchase German bonds from French banks which had previously purchased the securities under a repurchase transaction.

The general nature of the transactions involved in this scheme were 'German style' repurchase agreements, commonly referred to as sale and buy back trades. Under German law, reserves must be held against these transactions. In 1985 the German Bundesbank, which administers laws put forth by the federal banking supervisory board in Berlin, sent a letter to German banks stating that the practice of entering into 'false' or 'unreal' repos was illegal and improper. Under a 'false' repo, the seller of securities orally commits to repurchase the same issue at a forward date but does *not* send a confirmation or telex to the buyer of the forward obligation. This is done to mask the trade and avoid reserving against the second leg of the transaction. The practice of engaging in 'false' repos was rumoured to have been fairly widespread within the German banking system prior to the XYZ problem.

As stated, the XYZ situation is both complicated and unresolved by the courts. Therefore, in order to simplify our task we will examine only those elements of the affair which deal directly with financing transactions as short-term investments.

Traders at XYZ bank were apparently transacting 'false' repos with French banks. While the majority of trades were executed through both French and German money brokers, XYZ remained principal on all transactions with French counterparties. XYZ's traders would sell German sovereign bonds, called bunds, to French banks for regular settlement or on a one month forward basis with an oral commitment to buy back these same bunds in one month. The sale price of the securities was the current market price of the securities flat (i.e., without margin) and the repurchase price was the original price at the outset of the trade plus or minus the difference between the coupon rate on the bunds and the one month German money market rate. The pricing of the securities as described here is not different from that employed in most markets worldwide. However, when it came time to unwind the trade, XYZ usually rolled the contract for another month in a series of rollovers. While this practice is also not uncommon in the markets, XYZ required that the historical value of the securities as of the previous trade be used when working up sale and repurchase prices. Thus, no marking-to-market of securities occurred. Given the positively sloped yield curve in the German markets (i.e., lower short-term than longer-term rates) until late 1989, the pricing practice made sense for XYZ. By financing long-term assets with lower cost short-term funds in this interest rate environment, XYZ was earning money. In addition, by pricing rollovers using historical values, XYZ was buying back bunds at lower and lower prices. After a series of rollovers, XYZ would buy back securities at prices substantially below the current market, and then immediately sell such positions for a good profit. The French banks, which were using these financing transactions as short-term investments, received a healthy per transaction fee and were comfortable with the arrangement since XYZ enjoyed an untarnished reputation in the market-place. These fees were in addition to the interest income they received on their loans to XYZ.

The party quickly came to an end in the later part of 1989, when the German yield curve inverted (i.e., higher short-term than longer-term rates). Thus, as short-term rates rose above longer-term rates and XYZ continued to employ its rollover pricing formula, XYZ was forced to rollover transactions or repurchase securities at higher and higher prices! Anyone can see that in an inverted yield curve environment, with interest rates rising across-the-board and bund prices declining, this strategy was doomed.

In February of 1990, when senior management at XYZ became aware of the situation, they discovered that they were being asked to repurchase agreements at prices substantially above the current market. XYZ management was further dismayed to learn that several billion German Marks worth of securities were involved. Faced with huge losses and unable to find a proper paper trail for the transactions, XYZ announced it would not purchase these securities because its records only reflected a sale of such issues.

Senior management at XYZ was obviously unaware of the extent of these 'false repos'. Upon learning of the total exposure, a senior official at XYZ claimed that his traders were not authorised to make such repo commitments and that since the bank had nothing in writing confirming the repurchase obligation, it was not obligated to repurchase the securities.

After a brief period of confusion, XYZ agreed to repurchase securities while maintaining the right to claim money from the French banks for a period of one year if it was discovered that the blame lay outside the bank (i.e., with French counterparties). Note that although the incident was indeed unfortunate, no lender of cash lost money due to dealings with XYZ bank.

Who is to blame for this mini-meltdown of the international repo market? XYZ's management must share some of the responsibility for this situation, as their bank's trading operation obviously lacked proper internal controls, management information systems and audit procedures. To a lesser extent, the French banks involved in the trades would not have been in such a precarious position had they required a master repurchase agreement be signed with XYZ, insisted on timely telexes confirming the second leg of the transaction, and required that market prices be used in all trade rollovers.

As mentioned earlier, the US market for Repurchase Agreements experienced some hiccups in the 1980s due to a period of rapid growth coupled with a poor regulatory structure to police the markets and its participants. Since I view the international repo market today as being very similar to the US repo market of the early 1980s, we must closely examine market history so that previous mistakes may be avoided. Market disruptions such as those discussed within this chapter benefit no one, and need to be addressed *before* they occur. By transacting business in a prudent fashion we are able to take advantage of market opportunities with a minimum of default risk. In a broader context, repo market participants add critical liquidity to the global capital markets. Situations which jeopardise this function will likely result in a less than optimal allocation of global resources for the world economy. Here, the best medicine is preventive medicine!

SUGGESTED GUIDELINES FOR INVESTING IN 'REPURCHASE AGREEMENTS'

1. *Know your counterparty*
   - evaluate customer creditworthiness to ensure the highest possible degree of safety
   - only deal with reputable firms
2. *Accept delivery of collateral*
   - transfer collateral to your custodian bank or account at a central depository (Euro-clear or Cedel)
   - take physical possession if necessary
   - only transact on a hold-in-custody basis with well capitalised, reputable dealers and banks
3. *Require margin*
   - maintain proper margin by 'marking-to-market' collateral daily when transacting US style repos
4. *Require proper documentation*
   - execute a Master Repurchase Agreement contract with all counterparties of US style repos
   - receive trade confirmations and telexes on a timely basis
   - if transacting in sale/buyback arrangements, require confirmation of the forward obligation at the trade's inception
5. *Require accurate pricing of collateral*
   - full accrual pricing of collateral
   - market prices used in all transactions
   - independently confirm prices to ensure proper security

SUMMARY

The economic benefits of financing transactions are substantial for lenders of cash. While the repo markets have experienced some bumps and bruises in America and Europe over the years, the risk/reward analysis is greatly in favour of the investor when the business is done prudently. As the need to borrow currency against a wide range of international securities continues to grow, dealer appetite for such transactions as a source of funding will follow suit. As you proceed to become involved in all the markets discussed in this

Financing Transactions as Short-term Investments

book, remember we all have a vested interest in ensuring that past problems of the repo market are *not* repeated. Happy Hunting!

Sources

Wall Street Journal. Sept. 10, 1982. 'SEC to Reconsider Its Rules on Repurchase Agreements'.
Wall Street Journal. Aug. 26, 1982. 'S & P Affirms Ratings on 55 Issues Involving Lombard-Wall'.
Wall Street Journal. Aug. 19, 1982. 'Lombard-Wall Creditors Freed to Sell Collateral on Loans'.
Wall Street Journal. Aug. 17, 1982. 'Lombard-Failure May Cause Losses for Many N.Y. Agencies'.
Institutional Investor. Aug. 1982. 'Drysdale: What Really Happened'.
Dow Jones News Wire. May 25, 1982. 'Solomon Sees Drysdale Crisis Due to Market Practices'.
Barron's. May 24, 1982. 'How Drysdale Default Shook Wall Street'.
Wall Street Journal. May 21, 1982. 'Drysdale Trading Becomes Subject of SEC Investigation',
Wall Street Journal. May 20, 1982. 'Bond Markets: Treasury Yields Fall Amid Drysdale Crisis'.
Dow Jones News Wire. June 18, 1982. 'Chase Chief Says Drysdale Liability Hasn't been Defined'.
Barron's. Aug. 12, 1982. 'Drysdale Collapse Leaves Many Unresolved Problems'.
The Bond Buyer. Oct. 7, 1982. 'Two New York Banks Sue Drysdale Accountant, for Nearly 1 Billion'.
Wall Street Journal. April 17, 1986. 'ESM Co-Founders Plead Guilty to Conspiracy, Fraud'.
Wall Street Journal. May 3, 1984. 'Government-Bond Market, Once Dreary, Has Few Regulations and a Lot of Risk'.

Part II

1: Risks in International Securities Lending – Identification and Minimisation

Habib Motani, Clifford Chance, London

Although securities lending programmes give scope for enhancing the performance of an investment portfolio, inevitably that enhancement is not risk free. This needs to be borne in mind in particular by those who lend securities owned by others (such as trustees or managers of pension and other investment funds and custodians) because a failure to address these risks could result in claims against them by the owners of the securities.

This chapter seeks to identify the principal areas of risk and then suggest opportunities to minimise them. Total elimination of risk is unlikely to be possible. Even where risk cannot be eliminated, risk identification remains important to enable participants properly to assess their risk/reward profile.

ESSENTIAL ELEMENTS OF A SECURITIES LOAN

Before looking at the main types of risk and how to address them, it is worth analysing the main components of a securities lending transaction.

There are generally four significant commercial elements in a securities loan.

(1) The lender transfers the full ownership in the securities lent to the borrower. Usually, this is against a transfer to the lender by the borrower of collateral which will cover the value of the securities transferred.
(2) The commercial intention is that the lender should retain the income and other rights attaching to the securities transferred.
(3) Adjustments to the collateral may be necessary during the life of the loan to maintain the loan value to collateral value relationship established at the outset.
(4) At the end of the loan, the securities and the collateral are returned.

It will be apparent that the word 'loan' is something of a misnomer. The reality of the legal position is that the transfer of the securities lent is an outright 'transfer' rather than a 'loan'. The explanation for this lies in the purpose of the loan. The borrower's aim in borrowing is normally to permit him to settle a trade which he has entered into in the market. His market purchaser is therefore expecting to receive and become owner of the securities delivered in that settlement. The market purchaser is not interested in receiving securities over which some third party has rights.

As a result, the lending agreement will structure the transaction so that, from a legal point of view, the securities 'loan' will be an outright transfer of the securities lent, and the lender's right to a return of the lent securities will be a contractual right to receive back securities of the same type and number as those lent.

MAIN AREAS OF RISK

There are various ways of categorising the main risks involved in securities lending. The two main headings are *credit risk* and *operational risk*.

Credit risks include:

- counterparty risk,
- risks inherent in collateral,
- risks which arise because of a default.

Steps can be taken to minimise these risks. A lending agreement which recognises the risks and deals with them as far as possible is the most logical step.

Operational risks include:

- risks arising out of the settlement or delivery system being used,
- risks inherent in a party's own systems and control procedures,
- risks associated with the use of an agent bank or custodian,
- costs associated with the programme,
- regulatory requirements, and
- tax.

These risks are mainly more external risks. While risk management is possible with some of them, there will be a residue of risk which needs to be recognised but cannot really be eliminated.

CREDIT RISK

Counterparty Risk

We acknowledged at the beginning that a securities loan is better analysed as an outright transfer rather than a loan. The borrower's obligation to return the lent securities is therefore a contractual right of the lender to receive back equivalent securities (securities of the same type and number as those lent). If the borrower does not perform his obligation to deliver equivalent securities, the lender does not have a right to go and take the securities back. Instead, he has a breach of contract claim against the borrower.

As a result, if the borrower becomes insolvent, the lender will have a claim in the insolvency of the borrower, but no right to the securities themselves.

This counterparty risk applies equally to any claim regarding the income arising on lent securities (or on securities provided as collateral).

The right to receive dividends or coupon payments is normally attached to the ownership of the securities. By transferring ownership, the right to the income is also transferred. Any arrangement under which the borrower will pass that income back is a contractual arrangement. Where the borrower passes on a dividend, the dividend received by the lender is not a real dividend, it is a 'manufactured' one. If the borrower does not perform his obligation to pass on the income, the lender has only a claim for breach of contract against the borrower.

Voting rights are comparable but are more difficult to deal with. Most securities lending agreements either abandon the lender's voting rights or, at best, make only a weak attempt at retaining them. In practice, a lender's ability to exercise voting rights attaching to the lent securities will depend on the borrower having an equivalent amount of the relevant securities and complying with the lender's voting instructions.

In reality, the borrower probably will not have the relevant securities at the relevant time. Requiring a return of the securities lent is obviously not a very convenient alternative solution.

What if the lender suffers additional losses because of this? Borrowers are naturally reluctant to cover lenders for consequential loss. The lender is, therefore, at risk if, for example, he lends securities which have become the subject of a lucrative takeover bid and he finds that the borrower does not comply with his instructions to accept the offer in time. A worse position could be if the lender lends securities after he has committed them to an offer and the borrower fails to return them before the last time for acceptance of the offer and the offer lapses.

Collateral

The usual method of dealing with counterparty credit risk is to take 'collateral'. It is customary to take collateral of a value greater than the value of the securities lent (the difference being the margin).

Collateral can be taken in many forms, such as cash, guarantees, letters of credit and, frequently, alternative securities. Before looking at issues relating to the type of collateral utilised, let us look at an issue which has been the subject of a good deal of discussion recently in the London Market.

Clearly, for collateral to serve as a useful risk minimisation tool, it must be taken in a way which will be effective under the relevant law. The focus of the discussion that has recently taken place has been the question whether the mechanism utilised in some standard documentation for the taking of collateral gives rise to ineffective collateral security (on the basis that the particular security provided is in a form which, to be effective, requires security filings which are not in practice carried out). The collateral in question has been collateral in the form of other securities.

The result of the discussion has been the adoption of a different mechanism for taking collateral (not a new mechanism, because it is one which has been used previously in other documentation).

The revised mechanism works by dealing with the collateral securities in a similar way to the securities being lent. Thus, as with the securities being lent, there is an outright transfer of the collateral securities. The borrower's right to a return of the collateral securities is, therefore, a contractual right to securities equivalent to the securities forming those originally delivered as collateral.

The two contractual rights (i.e., that of the lender to a return of equivalent securities and that of the borrower to a return of equivalent collateral securities) are set off against each other, thereby protecting each party against the failure to perform, or the insolvency, of the other party. (Remember that the borrower also has a credit risk on the lender, and this mechanism therefore usefully serves as a risk management tool for the borrower as well as the lender.)

It has proved possible to achieve this where dealing with an agreement governed by English law and where the parties are both incorporated in the UK. However, although securities lending may be carried out on a global basis, one system of law does not always successfully operate on a global basis. For instance, even if a securities lending agreement is governed by a system of law which, like English law, will operate a set off along the lines mentioned in the event of a UK borrower's insolvency, the lender must ask whether the same result can be achieved where the borrower is incorporated in a different jurisdiction? English law will say that the rights of the lender in a borrower's insolvency will be affected by the law of the place of the borrower's incorporation. Lenders must, therefore, be prepared to obtain advice on the legal position in the place where the counterparty is incorporated or located.

In order to determine what the potential risks are of using different forms of collateral, various questions need to be asked about the specific collateral.

(i) *Valuation.* How easily can you value the collateral? Are frequent price reports received? Are they up to date when received? What is the issuer's credit rating and is this adequately reflected in the valuation?

What about the valuation of the securities lent? How easy is it to value them both for establishing the amount of collateral needed at the outset and for keeping the lender's margin cover under review?

What actually happens when price movements mean the lender no longer has full margin cover? If additional collateral is needed, how long before the lender asks for it and receives it? What is the mechanism whereby additional collateral is provided? Is it automatically provided or does the lender have to ask for it? How long could a lender be operating below its agreed collateral margin? Most lending agreements provide for adjustments to collateral to take place at the end of each business day by reference to the prices ruling at that time. Is the lender willing to take the risk of price volatility that can occur during the day?

(ii) *Exchange risk.* Where collateral is not in the same currency as the securities lent, there is in addition, an exchange risk. Does the collateral margin cover this?

(iii) *Income cover.* Does the collateral margin cover simply the value of the securities lent or does it also cover the borrower's contractual obligation to account for dividends and income on the securities lent? With fixed income securities the income element can be a relatively significant amount.

(iv) *Limitations of the collateral.* The collateral itself may have limitations built into it. For example a letter of credit may have an expiry time. What is your cover between expiry and the return of your securities or delivery of fresh collateral? Is it practical to obtain cover for that period?

The collateral may also be affected because it is subject to the rights of the clearance or depositary system in which it is held.

For example, Euroclear's rules give Euroclear rights to securities held within Euroclear to secure monies owed to Euroclear. As a result, Euroclear might have first claim against collateral which the lender is expecting to be delivered to him.

All of these items relating to collateral are ones where the lender can protect himself through a proper approach to valuation, to the type of collateral accepted, to the level of the collateral margin and to the counterparty limits which it sets, market practices permitting. If market practices do not permit, then again some judgement on the risks and rewards of the business will be called for.

DEFAULT

The true value of collateral is not its price, but what it will be worth when it has to be realised to cover a default. This, and default in general, raises such a number of significant risk questions that it is worth considering them separately.

The first question for a lender is 'does the lending agreement give him a right to deal with the collateral fully and freely?' Because this is such a fundamental question, my preference is for lending agreements to provide for an absolute transfer of legal ownership to collateral and for all the necessary documents of title, transfer forms etc. to have been delivered up front. This is the best way of ensuring for the lender this freedom to deal.

The alternative approach of treating collateral as a pure security interest (such as a charge or pledge, where, for example, the borrower retains some ownership rights in the collateral, most notably the right to the return of the specific asset pledged or charged if he discharges the loan) can cause difficulties in practice.

For instance, in the UK the holder of a security interest can find himself blocked from enforcing his security if the borrower goes into administration, a form of insolvency procedure similar to Chapter 11 in the US. In some jurisdictions there is also a strict duty to realise an asset taken as security at the best possible price.

These considerations make it important to take full ownership rights over the collateral where possible. It is part of the basic question: 'Can I, the lender, deal with this asset as if it were my own, notwithstanding the fact that I have a contractual obligation to deliver back an equivalent asset at the end of the loan?'

Other practical questions also arise. For example, if the collateral is in the form of securities, will the lender be able to sell them quickly? How will the sale be effected? Do the officers of the lender who will actually have to organise the sale know what to do? Will they sell through a broker? Which broker? What does the broker need? Does he need transfer forms? Where does one find these forms?

Suppose that the collateral is a guarantee. How is it called? Do you have to give a notice? What form of notice? Does the guarantee give the guarantor a grace period? How long?

What about any local law requirements? Are there local law procedures you have to comply with? For example, if you have foreign equities as collateral, are there any legal requirements of the country of the equities which you need to comply with?

These questions may seem obvious. But if the first time people start asking them is after a default has taken place then the circumstances may well provoke a longer lead time in answering them than might otherwise be the case. Meanwhile of course the market prices of the collateral may be moving.

In a default situation lenders need to think, too, about buying-in securities to cover themselves for the borrower's failure to return. How easily can you buy in your securities? How liquid is the issue? What happens if you cannot buy-in? Will similar securities be usable? Does the lending agreement give you an indemnity against the extra costs incurred in effecting a buy-in, on top of the value of the collateral you hold? I mentioned earlier that borrowers are reluctant to agree to cover consequential loss, but it should be possible for a lender to negotiate in a provision for reasonable costs incurred in respect of a buy-in.

OPERATIONAL RISKS

Settlement and Delivery Risks

Lenders need to consider whether the settlement or delivery system they use to settle the securities loan or collateral transfer imposes risks on them. For example, do you have to part with the securities before you receive the collateral? Do you have a daylight exposure?

This will obviously happen where settlement of the securities transfer and settlement of the collateral transfer takes place in different time zones. Japanese equities versus UK stock, for example.

Some lenders refuse to accept daylight exposure (particularly trustees who are under fiduciary duties). Current London Market Stock Exchange standard form documentation effectively gives the lender an option. It is drafted on the basis that simultaneous deliveries are required but the parties may waive that requirement when required to meet market practice. Lenders who will not accept daylight exposure may take a temporary deposit of cash collateral until the securities collateral is delivered. That is, however, likely to result in a reduced return on the securities loan, a factor that must be weighed against the risk of daylight exposure.

Systems and Controls Procedures

Lenders must consider whether their internal systems and control procedures carry risks. Questions which should be asked include:

- When you lend securities how accurate and up to date is your own 'inventory' of the securities you have available to lend?
- How good is your monitoring of values?
- How good is your reaction time in asking for more collateral?
- If there is a default, how geared up are you to reacting and getting hold of securities from alternative sources or realising collateral?
- Do your officers who will implement the realisation of collateral and the buying-in know what to do? (Have you had a 'fire drill'?)
- Are you tracking ownership entitlements associated with the securities on loan. For example, if you have equities on loan and there is an issue of shares to shareholders, will you pick this up? Do you have procedures to ensure you will not lend out securities on which you have just accepted a takeover offer for delivery to the bidder next week?
- If a dividend or a coupon is paid on securities on loan will you get immediate value on it or will you only receive value several days after it was paid? If so are you compensated?

Agent Bank/Custodian

Where securities lenders operate through agent banks or custodians, these operational questions need to be asked in relation to the agent bank or custodian. How good is its monitoring and valuing and coupon tracking etc? How quickly will it react on a default?

What are the agent bank's principles in establishing counterparty credit limits? Do they fit the lender's own requirements? If the lender needs to buy-in securities because the borrower has failed to return them, how effective is the agent bank likely to be at finding an alternative source of supply?

Costs, Regulatory Requirements, Tax

Finally, there are three items categorised as operational risks:

- costs
- regulatory requirements
- tax

They are risks because anything which increases costs or externally imposes procedural requirements is a risk, whether it is a direct cost or, like compliance costs, an indirect one.

There is no purpose served in looking at these items in detail here, because individual parties in individual countries are going to be subject to different cost structures and different regulatory and tax regimes. These are, nevertheless, risks which should be reviewed by potential lenders at the country level at the outset.

CONCLUSION

In conclusion, I have sought to bring out the risks involved in securities lending by looking at them under the headings of credit risk and operational risks, by asking some of the questions which potential participants need to ask of themselves to see where the risks are for themselves, and to highlight approaches which will help in seeking to minimise these risks.

The risks which are particularly important to bear in mind when lending on a global basis are:

- foreign exchange risk
- daylight exposure
- foreign law requirements and
- realisation procedures involving foreign jurisdictions

Strategies for controlling credit risks are familiar and include setting appropriate counterparty limits, choosing collateral carefully, taking collateral effectively and, wherever feasible, building in adequate set-off arrangements.

In the case of operational risks:

- to the extent that they are your internal risks, you may be able to control them by ensuring that your internal procedures are fully established, efficient and familiar to your officers who are involved;
- to the extent they are external, there may be little which can be done to minimise them. They should, however, at least be recognised and taken into account in assessing the appropriateness of individual transactions as well as of particular securities lending programmes.

2: Global Custody
Daniel R. Roccato, Morgan Stanley, London

In order to fully appreciate the concept of global custody it is useful to consider the many varied financial instruments available to an investor in only one market such as Japan or the UK. These include equities in all configurations, fixed income securities with variable and fixed coupons, a myriad of derivative products including securities options and currency options, 'baskets' of securities based on a particular index, and unit trusts.

The complexity of these instruments can then be taken a step further when thought of in terms of cross-border transactions. Suddenly, a new regulatory, political, and risk analysis needs to be considered in addition to the basic investment decision. Perhaps even more profound is the effect of transacting business in a currency unit other than one's own.

Finally, local practices, customs, and culture are factors which investors would not think twice about in a domestic setting, but which can have a significant impact on the success of the foreign investment. Though much can be made of 'globalisation' and state-of-the-art communications systems, it would be a serious error of judgement to underestimate these intangible aspects.

A 'global custodian' attempts to bring order and clarity to this landscape. A narrow definition of custody would be a service provided to investors for the settlement and safekeeping of securities and cash investments. We have moved beyond this rather limited mission and evolved into 'global securities services' which expands the range of services to include value-added products such as multi-currency portfolio reporting, cash management, foreign exchange, assured payment schemes and securities lending.

It is interesting to note that global custody existed long before an image or a particular vernacular was created for it. Banks, predominantly based in Switzerland, the UK and the USA, have been in the global custody business for decades without explicitly identifying the product as a differentiating service. Like so many successful products before it, global custody has been presented as a new service, almost revolutionary, invented to fill a real void in the marketplace.

While we admit that global custody can trace its roots back to the early days of cross-border securities investment, the product itself has become more complex through the evolution into the wider realm of securities services.

The integration of these add-on services has reduced the need for separate vendors. Even in those instances where the services are 'unbundled' among several providers, the global custodian is fully expected to be able to be the one point of commonality between the vendors. Today, clients are demanding that the custodian be flexible enough, structurally and technically, to absorb data from various sources, process the data, and present the client with timely and accurate information which can assist them throughout the investment management process.

FUNCTIONS OF A GLOBAL CUSTODIAN

The core set of functions for a global custodian are the settlement and safekeeping of international securities. It is only from these basic tasks that additional services may evolve.

Settlement

First and foremost, investors expect their custodian to effectively perform the settlement function. To accomplish this, the custodian may utilise a branch office, a transnational clearing organisation such as Euroclear, a direct relationship with the domestic securities depository, or a local agent bank which can be described as a 'subcustodian'. The mixture of these relationships across borders comprises the custodian's 'network'.

Settlement refers to both the transfer of securities and the movement of cash associated with it. There are two possible scenarios: a securities movement accompanied by a simultaneous transfer of cash, or a securities movement independent of the cash transfer. As countries continue their implementation of the Group of 30 recommendations, it is clear that the settlement function has become less complex. Investors are at the point where they consider efficient settlement in the major capital markets a non-negotiable aspect of custodial services.

Safekeeping

Following the successful settlement of a transaction, it is necessary to hold the securities in 'safekeeping'. The safekeeping function, as the name implies, is the protection of the integrity of the asset. This includes protection against theft, destruction and fraud.

Assets are usually not static. Instead, there are activities associated with ownership of securities such as dividend and income payments, proxy voting, changes in capitalisation and tender offers. We can define this component of safekeeping as securities administration. The efficiency of this function is highly dependent on local market practice, regulatory environment, level of technology, and choice of subcustodian relationship.

Building on these functions, custodians have expanded their product lines to include more value-added services such as tax reclamation, cash management, foreign exchange, guaranteed payment schemes, portfolio analysis (performance measurement), and securities lending. All of these activities are information-based in that timeliness and quality of information flows are critical to their successful delivery.

Information Management

The very foundation of global custody as a product is based on the availability, processing, and reporting of information. This is one distinct area where global custodians can bring clear value to the table. The speed and accuracy of this information is crucial to the investor. Thus, custodians continue to develop enhanced delivery methods utilising the latest technology.

The reporting function ranges in scope from very basic trade status and portfolio information to sophisticated valuations and performance measurements against a recognised benchmark. The real value-added is that custodians collect information from several sources, located in many countries, in different formats, which cover a variety of securities, and present a comprehensive standardised report to the client. At an even higher level, custodians provide the raw data to the client's computer allowing the client to manipulate the information as needed.

Increasingly, custodians have gone beyond paper based communication methods and are developing customised computer links with their clients which enhances the exchange of data within a secure environment. The drive toward automation has resulted in unprecedented close relationships between clients and custodians resulting in a highly customised service.

For their part, investors have begun to realize that custodians as providers of information, can be strategic partners in their overall success.

Network Management

The need for local support and representation in each market where they provide a service is critical to a global custodian. There is no better example

Global Custody

where you are only as good as your weakest link. As everything in this business can be ultimately traced back to a country level event, whether it be a trade, corporate reorganisation, coupon payment, etc., a high quality network of subcustodial relationships is essential.

Realising this, custodians devote enormous resources to selecting, managing and evaluating subcustodians. This task is usually the responsibility of a dedicated network management team. The network function should begin with in-depth country analysis which includes an assessment of the regulatory environment, market organisation and infrastructure, risk assessment, and identification of potential subcustody providers.

Selection of the subcustodian needs to be based on objective factors such as service quality, compatibility of technology, business strategy of the subcustodian, and economics. Following selection and implementation, including technology, the network management group will have the task of evaluating the service standards, organising on-site due diligence reviews of each local market, and working with the subcustodian to continually improve quality.

Value-Added Services – Securities Lending

In response to their clients needs, and in pursuit of enhanced profitability, providers of global custody are expanding their service offerings to include 'value-added' items such as cash management, performance measurement, and perhaps most notably securities lending.

Securities lending is perhaps the most tangible aspect of a custodian providing a service which gives the client identifiable incremental portfolio return. There are two types of securities lending facilities provided by leading global custodians. In a **directed** program, the client actively manages every aspect of the securities loan including identifying and negotiating rates with borrowers, collecting dividends, managing collateral, and instructing the custodian to receive or deliver the securities.

In a client-directed program, the custodians' primary role is one of settlement agent for the securities loan activity. However, it is possible that the custodian will have systems robust enough to identify these transactions as loans, as opposed to normal trades, and continue to include them in the overall portfolio reporting package.

Depending on the client's strategy, it may be more appropriate to take advantage of the custodian's **discretionary** securities lending program. Unlike the directed program where the client manages nearly all aspects of the lending activity, in a discretionary program, the custodian assumes overall responsibility. The client will identify which assets are 'lendable' and will often approve the ultimate borrowers. Only those custodians with a proven global distribution capability, stringent internal procedures and controls, and sophisticated systems will be able to provide an integrated service whereby client involvement is minimized and returns are maximized. For their efforts, custodians share in the actual revenue earned as a result of the program.

Given the inherent difficulty involved with implementing a successful securities lending service, custodians may form strategic partnerships with external parties or the clients themselves to accomplish the task. Perhaps more than any sevice, the implementation of a securities lending program further solidifies the long-term partnership of custody relationships.

EVOLUTION OF GLOBAL CUSTODY

Early Stages

We can identify four distinct periods in the evolution of global custody: pre-1980, separation from traditional banking, product distinction and competition and expansion.

Prior to the late 1970s, global custody lacked a well-defined image. While banks routinely held international assets for cross-border investors, there was no label attached to the product. Externally, global custody was facilitated by a network of traditional correspondent banking ties carefully cultivated through decades of international finance activity.

There were no marketing campaigns, no network management teams, and certainly no stand-alone business units within the banks. It was a service provided upon request to a banking client rather than a product marketed to either existing or new clients.

Separation from Traditional Banking Functions

During the late 1970s and into the early 1980s, several banks, perhaps cognisant of the potential risk and uniqueness of the securities business, organised global custody as a separate function.

Securities administration departments came into being. These departments were distinct from traditional banking areas and staff began to develop expertise in aspects of securities processing. The environment, however, remained doggedly 'backoffice'.

Product Distinction

With the increase of cross-border investment, banks slowly became aware of the product potential of global custody, complete with risks and rewards.

The business itself was devoted to the settlement of international securities transactions and the collection of income.

Trade settlement became a big and visible issue. As foreign investors discovered new markets, the various settlement systems began to crack under the pressure. Thus banks began to differentiate themselves in the market along the lines of international settlement performance. The global custody business became attractive to banks in that it was a fee-based oligopoly. Perhaps best of all, profits could be made through recognised market inefficiencies.

Following the rapid expansion and deregulation of the international capital markets, investors became less willing to limit themselves to domestic returns. Securities firms sought to capitalise on this fundamental change by building expertise and capacity which would enable them to meet investors' demands for international research and execution.

Finally, sophisticated trading strategies, developed in the USA and based on technology, were being successfully exported. Despite market setbacks along the way, the international investment boom was in high gear by the end of the decade.

At first, global custodians were caught off-guard and responded accordingly. Lack of foresight, perhaps owing to the back-office image, meant that a massive investment in systems and people was needed to keep pace with a hitherto predictable and stable client base. In some cases the sheer size of the banks and lack of expertise prevented quick decisive action. Thus, the race began.

Competition and Expansion

In any industry where a gap exists between the needs of a client and the ability of vendors to satisfy that need, opportunity exists for new entrants. The market dynamics for new entrants were further enhanced by the existing oligopoly of providers and corresponding lack of differentiation.

However, despite these positive characteristics, significant entry barriers existed. Increasingly, global custody has become dependent on information technology. Rapid communication with clients and subcustodians required global data networks linking mainframes and PCs have to be implemented. Extensive knowledge of each local market is also needed to ensure control and minimise investor risk. Client expectations have also increased dramatically, moving away from efficient settlement, to include sophisticated portfolio reporting, cash management and revenue enhancement through securities lending.

Within this environment, international investment banks, perhaps most notably Morgan Stanley, moved to capitalise on the opportunity. Building off a platform of international securities trading expertise and massive investments in technology, these organisations marshalled their operational capabilities into a global custody product.

With increased competition, global custody providers have begun to differentiate their services based on performance and client services, expand the number of services offered, and perhaps most predictably, develop sophisticated marketing programmes.

The evolution of global custody from a secondary backwater banking service to a high-tech stand-alone revenue generator in large part can be attributed to marketing. It could be argued that a small group of bankers, predominantly British and American, took a traditional European banking function, dressed it up, gave it a slick veneer, and sold it to the world.

Indications are that the current period has a fair amount of life left in it. There is still plenty of room for added 'bells and whistles', more product differentiation, and still more marketing. There are, however, indications that the next phase of development is approaching. This will be marked by industry consolidation and strategic alliances as weaker providers find themselves unable to continue the required levels of investment spending. The rate and magnitude of competitive dislocation could be accelerated by the precarious financial condition of many of the leading custodians.

IMAGE

A lot can be said for the word 'image' in any service business. Whether describing a retail store, airline, or a restaurant, service companies need to constantly project and maintain an image. Global custodians have become aware that marketplace perception, on the part of clients, subcustodians, and independent intermediaries (consultants, brokers, fund managers, etc.), is critical to success.

The image of global custody has followed a similar pattern to the American automobile. Henry Ford developed a mass produced automobile, the Model T, which was designed to meet a growing nation's insatiable desire for mobility. The car was intended to transport people without much fanfare. The car offered no options and was only available in one colour – black.

Once the need for basic transportation was met, it was not long before new entrants began to differentiate their products along the lines of luxury and performance. (For a long time, Henry Ford refused to modify his existing design and indeed jeopardised the future of his company.) Eventually marketing campaigns were created, expanded, and fine-tuned to target specific consumers who increasingly demanded more functionality. The product was forever changed.

Similarly, we have witnessed global custody transformed from a nondescript back-office function to an essential sophisticated financial service product. Gaining this status has had a positive effect on the industry by raising the level of professionalism and overall standards. Overall, this has had a positive impact on clients who have seen service standards rise accordingly.

More than anything else, the staff of the global custodian is the principal purveyor of image. While a strong network, state of the art technology, and a long-term commitment to the business, are essential components for success, the quality and responsiveness of the global custodian's staff is the crown jewel. As in any service business, clients want to deal with competent enthusiastic people. Further, it is important that these people have the support of senior management, are empowered to make relationship-oriented decisions and are rewarded accordingly for their efforts.

Pushed by clients and driven by competition, the global custody industry will continue to evolve. This transformation will include a move toward integrated securities services with less emphasis on settlement and safekeeping, competition from new entrants, consolidation among existing providers, and ever more value-added services. Providing information, which forms the basis of value-added services such as securities lending, will require a sustained investment in technology and even closer cooperation between the client and their custodial partner. Responsiveness and flexibility, both technically and organisationally, will be required as clients themselves increase their demands and expectations.

3: The Function of the Clearing House

Securities Lending in an International Clearing System: Cedel's Securities Lending Programme
Susan Alexander, Cedel, Luxembourg

Introduction

A grim statistic is often cited whenever specialists in international securities gather. The figure is that 40 per cent of all transactions in global markets fail to settle on the contractual date; some pundits put the percentage even higher. While the exact number may be difficult to verify, what can be readily determined is that many of these failures are due to the inability of the seller to deliver the securities to the buyer by the trade's settlement date.

The resulting costs of these failures go beyond any simple claim the buyer may make. As cash sits un-utilised and the coupon (if the security is a bond) accrues, both front and back office staff spend time and money trying to resolve the problem. Compounding the difficulty is the fact that one failure frequently leads to others. As subsequent trades dependent on the receipt of the original securities fail, a chain reaction is set off and the misery spreads.

Cedel, the European-based international clearing system, was established over twenty years ago to facilitate an orderly settlement process in the nascent Eurobond markets. Once organised, Cedel was naturally placed to know if settlement would fail to occur because of securities being unavailable, as well as to identify potential sources of the needed issue. Securities lending in the form of stock loan and government bond 'repos' (repurchase agreements) was well established in the United States and some other national markets. Developing a securities lending service as a means of averting fails was an obvious product to offer to customers.

Consequently, Cedel's securities lending programme, now more than a decade old, developed as a result both of its role in facilitating settlements and its being uniquely positioned to offer the service. As a clearing house, Cedel's business is providing the market with two basic services: settlement of trades and custody of securities. Because of the former, Cedel is essentially the first to know when a trade is failing due to the counterparty's lacking the necessary securities. Because of the latter, Cedel also knows who holds the needed issue. Putting the two halves together by arranging the loan of the securities for a fee was a matter of simple logic. Exactly how the service developed and its basic characteristics reflect the essential nature of the problem and the attributes of the institution providing the solution.

The settlement procedure in Cedel involves the processing of instructions received from customers through various forms of telecommunications media (primarily the General Electric and SWIFT networks as well as telex). Once Cedel's main computer completes the processing of all transactions due to settle on a particular day, trades which will fail to settle due to a lack of the securities in the counterparty's account are identified. By arranging a loan of the necessary securities, Cedel can enable the trade to settle on time.

Types of Borrowers and Lenders

An institution opening a Cedel account can apply to participate in several forms of securities borrowing and lending. The customer may be:

— an automatic lender, meaning that all securities in the account are available for lending on an ongoing basis;
— an automatic borrower, who is a customer who always wants to borrow securities whenever such a borrow would avert a trade's failure;
— a case-by-case lender, whose permission is required for each specific loan;
— a case-by-case borrower, who has been approved for borrowing but must request a borrow before one is made.

How It Works

At the completion of the processing cycle (currently at dawn each morning), trades which are going to fail because the required securities are unavailable have been identified. (The reverse of this situation, trades failing because funds are unavailable, is covered by another group of products which provide customers with short- and longer-term financing capabilities.)

If the seller is an automatic borrower and the securities are available for lending, a loan of the required securities is opened and the trade settles on time.

If an automatic borrower needs securities which are not available from an automatic lender, but the securities are available in the account of a case-by-case lender, the lender is asked if the securities can be borrowed and if possible a loan is opened.

Finally, customers who are case-by-case borrowers can phone or fax to request specific loans. If the securities are available on an automatic basis, a loan is arranged; if the lender is case-by-case, permission is sought.

Loan Duration

All loans are currently made on an overnight basis and extended each day as needed (or as is possible), with most loans lasting an average of two to three days. Typically by that time the securities which were originally required have appeared in the borrower's account and the loan is closed.

Loan Termination

Loans are usually terminated by the borrower with the return of the securities. In addition, the lender always has the right to call the loan. In about 50 per cent of cases when the lender needs the securities returned, another lender's securities can be substituted without the borrower needing to be informed. In most other cases, the borrower is notified that the loan is being terminated and is able to return the securities within a brief period of time.

According to the contractual lending agreement, a fourteen-day notice period of a loan recall is required. In reality, however, a lender rarely has to wait that long for the securities to be returned. The syndicate of banks who guarantee the loan (see below) may also request the termination of a loan. In this instance, the loan is considered to be terminated immediately.

Upon the loan's termination, the borrowed securities are returned to the lender's account and the lending fee is credited to the lender's account. The borrower is charged the fee, and the collateral which was being held against the loan is freed.

Credit Risk Management

Controlling credit risk is a crucial concern in any lending programme. The lender has exposure to the borrower of the securities. The borrower has exposure to the lender in the amount of the collateral. In Cedel, as mentioned above, a syndicate of banks provides a guarantee for the loaned securities. At the present time, syndicate members are: Citibank NA, Brussels, the lead manager; Banque Bruxelles Lambert SA, Brussels; Banque Générale du Luxembourg, Luxembourg; Banque Internationale à Luxembourg, Luxembourg; Crédit Commercial de France, Paris; Kredietbank NV, Brussels; Kredietbank SA Luxembourgeoise, Luxembourg; and Union Bank of Switzerland, Zurich.

The lender therefore can accept the combined creditworthiness of the syndicate rather than having to review and monitor each specific borrower.

In the event of a borrower's default, the syndicate will return to the lender either the same amount of the specific securities or cash equivalent to the market value of the securities loaned on the day of default, plus accrued interest and/or coupon and lending fees.

Collateral

Borrowers must undergo a credit review by Cedel and a committee of syndicate members. If satisfactory, a borrowing limit is established. Cash and securities held in the borrower's account serve as the collateral for the loans. Acceptance of a security as collateral is also based on the issue's credit. Collateral is valued as follows:

Bonds	90 per cent of market value
Convertibles	75 per cent of market value
Equities	66 per cent of market value
Warrants	0 per cent (i.e., not accepted)

Anonymity

Since the lender has accepted the guarantee of the syndicate, and the borrower has agreed to Cedel's monitoring of the collateral, anonymity can be preserved between borrower and lender. This is a benefit valued highly by both borrowers and lenders, who prefer that portfolio holdings and borrowing needs are kept confidential.

Fees

Lending rates are fixed according to currency. Deutschemark, Netherlands guilder, Japanese yen and Swiss franc denominated securities cost the borrower 2.50 per cent and earn the lender 1.50 per cent. Other currencies, such as US dollars and British pounds, cost 3.75 per cent and pay 2.75 per cent. An exception is Bank of England ECU-denominated T-bills, which are

1.875 per cent and 1 per cent respectively. The difference in borrowing and lending rates reflects the cost of the syndicate guarantee.

There is no charge for participating in the service, other than a fixed $8.00 transaction fee charged to the borrower for each loan.

Prioritisation

Cedel's goal in its bond lending service is to avert the maximum number of fails by lending the maximum amount of securities possible, thus benefiting the largest number of both borrowers and lenders. Currently, loans are made on the following basis.

When an automatic borrower needs the loan of a security, the system identifies the six automatic lenders with the largest positions in that particular issue. Securities from each of the six are borrowed in proportion to their holdings. For instance, assume that a borrower requires the loan of 6,000,000 (nominal value) of a bond and that the six automatic lenders with the largest positions in that security also each have 6,000,000. The system will then take 1,000,000 from each lender to make up the loan.

Lenders naturally desiring to collect fees on their portfolios want to quantify their expectations. Generally, larger positions are more lendable; smaller, odd lots are loaned less frequently. There tends to be greater demand for more recent issues; the bonds listed monthly as the most actively traded issues are also the ones for which the most demand exists. 'Hot' issues tend to include new issue eurobonds, recent sovereign issues and any issues which are deliverable into a futures contract or have options or other derivative instruments based on them which provide arbitrage opportunities. A 'cheapest to deliver' Bundesrepublik bond always has loan demand.

The Lender's Advantages

Why lend securities? The answer is primarily to receive fee income. With investors becoming more and more demanding in terms of performance, lending allows a portfolio manager to increase return with an acceptable degree of risk without needing to sell options, lower the credit quality of investments or employ other speculative strategies.

The lender can recall loans and is not committed for a fixed period. Using a clearing system gives the lender access to a large number of borrowers, while limiting the credit concern to the guarantee syndicate. Administration of the loan is minimal – a key concern from the lender's point of view because the fees generated can easily be offset by the costs of overseeing the programme. Cedel monitors the collateral and the customer receives daily reports on all lending activity in the account. Also, despite the discussion above about 'hot' issues, there remains the possibility for lenders with smaller positions in less active issues to generate income due to the odd settlement fail. Finally, the lender is not charged custody fees for securities on loan, increasing the overall attractiveness of lending.

The Borrower's Advantages

Besides the obvious benefit of averting fails, a clearing system programme offers access to a large pool of lenders. The availability of an issue can be determined and a loan consummated quickly and efficiently. Account positions serve as collateral; the borrower's administration and credit concerns are minimised.

Current Situation

The recent explosion of interest in securities lending and increased borrowing demand is due to a change of focus in the market. From a product primarily used to avert settlement failures, lending has evolved into a critical component of many trading strategies and a crucial part of sophisticated financing techniques. Lending has moved from 'back office' to 'front office' as futures, warrants and funding books all require taking 'short' positions, i.e., selling securities one does not own. Eventually, of course, delivery must occur; hence the need for borrowing. Borrowers in these situations have very different requirements from traditional 'fail' borrowers. The following attempts to compare the major differences between 'fail' lending (as provided by a clearing system) and 'direct' lending (so called because borrowers negotiate loans directly with lending institutions).

> Purpose: Avert fails versus facilitate trading strategies and trading desk financing
> Mode: Automatic versus negotiated
> Fees: Fixed versus market/negotiated
> Credit Assurance: Syndicate guarantee backed by account collateral versus individual monitoring and collateral management
> Confidentiality: Anonymous versus transparent
> Duration: Overnight versus fixed period
> Commitment: Subject versus pre-commitment ('icing')

In direct lending, loans are usually negotiated individually, with the term fixed and a fee reflecting current levels of interest rates and demand for the security agreed with the lender. Lender and borrower are known to each other; each establishes the other's creditworthiness and monitors credit lines. Types of acceptable collateral, its valuation and margining are also mutually agreed upon between borrower and lender.

As traders must often know whether a security can be borrowed before initiating a position, lenders can be asked to pre-commit to a loan before it is actually established. Banks and brokers with substantial on-going borrowing needs will sign contracts with large institutional investors ensuring exclusive access to a portfolio, sometimes with a guarantee of lending income. In these cases, lending is done on a virtually automatic basis and is one of the few points of similarity between direct lending and the lending offered by a clearing system.

New Developments

While the direct lending market has been evolving, clearing system lending has not been stagnant. It, too, is changing. From an original 'all or nothing', black/white approach, now automatic lenders can be increasingly specific about how their portfolios are loaned, making lending more attractive. Lenders can specify that loans be made only to certain borrowers and that other borrowers be excluded. Lenders may also indicate that only certain currencies in the portfolio be loaned, or that only a certain percentage of a position is available. Positions can also be excluded from lending.

The Future

As direct lending grows, so does the issue of whether a clearing system should also offer a lending service that supports securities lending on more than a 'fails' basis. At the same time that automation has made little human intervention necessary to process loans, there is pressure to offer 'brokered' or 'intermediary' lending in which loan terms and rates would be negotiated but the anonymity of borrower and lender preserved. While market demand certainly exists for such a service, and a clearing system could offer the benefits of confidentiality and administrative efficiency, it is not a role in which a clearing house traditionally has great experience. Ultimately, a business decision must be made as to the appropriateness and profitability, as well as potential risks, in developing such a business. While the possibility is certainly attractive, the appropriateness of the activity is an open question.

Meanwhile, the existing parameters of the clearing house service will continue to offer many benefits to both borrowers and lenders. For borrowers, it continues to be a major help in averting fails; it can also be a significant resource for specific borrowing requests. For lenders, it offers an

The Function of the Clearing House

efficient, 'user friendly' way to begin a securities lending programme and also provides the opportunity to earn fee income on positions which would otherwise be generating custody costs. Finally, regardless of whether an intermediary lending programme is implemented, improvements will continue to be made in traditional lending to avert fails for borrowers and reduce costs for lenders.

4: The Euroclear System
Martine Dinne, Euroclear Operations Centre, Brussels

Purpose of a Clearance and Settlement System

The purpose of securities clearance and settlement is to administer the exchange of money and securities between parties to a securities trade. Clearance is the process of determining accountability for the exchange of assets and establishes obligations for securities and funds due. Settlement is the completion of a trade wherein securities and, depending on the system, the corresponding funds are delivered and credited to the appropriate accounts. Each trade has two sides: a securities side and a cash side. The securities side concerns the transfer of securities and is the traditional activity of a clearance system. The cash side concerns the transfer of funds corresponding to the securities trade.

Clearance and settlement is a core process underlying the working of any securities market. Experience demonstrates that effective clearance and settlement is a necessary condition for an efficient securities market.

The clearance and settlement process requires the cooperation of a number of institutional intermediaries that might be involved in, or affected by, the transaction. Institutional intermediaries include, amongst others: banks, broker-dealers, custodians, central banks and other clearance systems. Cash countervalues of securities trades are settled in different ways depending on the system. Some systems settle the cash side of the transaction simultaneously with the securities side, others have various arrangements with cash settlement systems to provide for payment for transactions.

Securities clearance and settlement systems serve primarily financial institutions which may or may not be the ultimate owners of the securities involved in the transactions. The role of the clearance and settlement system is to reduce the cost, complexity and risk of delivering securities in settlement of a trade. If the parties to a trade agree to settle 'against payment' within a clearance and settlement system that offers against payment settlement, the role of the system is to eliminate counterparty risk related to the settlement of the trade.

Clearance and Settlement

If the parties to a trade use a clearance system only for the securities side, the transaction is said to be 'free of payment' because the cash side is arranged between the trading parties outside the clearance system. When a clearance system handles both the securities side and the cash side of a trade, or cash and securities settlement are coordinated between cash and securities systems, a transaction may be 'against payment' because the clearance system provides for the exchange of securities received from the seller for cash received from the buyer.

Broadly, there are two kinds of clearance systems, national and international. National clearance systems have different organisational characteristics. Some are governmentally created or administered organisations integrated into national banking systems. Others are private-sector associations created and operated by the members of securities exchanges or groups of securities exchanges.

National clearance systems serve national securities markets by providing clearance and settlement for domestically issued debt and equity securities and, increasingly, for issues of foreign corporations or supranational organisations that are traded in the local market, either on a stock exchange or over-the-counter. National clearance systems generally provide clearance and settlement only for trades settled in their own national currency. Some also provide clearance and settlement for trades denominated in widely-used composite currencies such as the European Currency Unit (ECU).

There are two major international clearance and settlement systems, the Brussels-based Euroclear System and Luxembourg-based CEDEL (Centrale de Livraison de Valeurs Mobilières SA). Both serve professionals active in securities markets internationally. The international clearance and settlement systems provide multicurrency clearance and settlement services and other related services for securities traded in a wide variety of national and composite currencies.

The Euroclear System: Profile and History

The Euroclear System is the largest clearance and settlement system for internationally-traded securities. Since its inception in 1968, it has been a catalyst for change and growth and it has been instrumental in the development of international securities markets. From the start, the Euroclear System has been based on the concept of simultaneous book-entry against payment settlement, in lieu of physical movement of securities.

The Euroclear System has more than 2600 participants worldwide, all of which are banks, broker-dealers or other regulated professionals engaged in managing new issues of securities, market-making, trading or administering portfolios from among the wide variety of securities accepted in the System.

Euroclear participants can confirm, clear and settle trades by book-entry in any of 30 currencies on a simultaneous delivery against payment (DVP) basis. Once securities are delivered against payment in the Euroclear System, settlement is final. DVP settlement minimises risks to participants.

The markets served by the Euroclear System are diverse. Nearly 42,000 different securities are accepted, covering a broad range of internationally traded fixed and floating rate debt instruments, convertibles, warrants and equities. This total includes domestic securities from more than 20 countries.

Securities are immobilised in an extensive network of depositary banks, national clearance systems and central banks. The depositary network also provides links with domestic markets for external deliveries and receipts of securities, thereby reducing risks involved in cross-border settlement.

The efficiency of the Euroclear settlement process is enhanced by such features as automated securities lending and borrowing to minimise settlement failure, and multicurrency money transfer. Extensive custody services simplify participants' portfolio administration.

In 1975, the Euroclear Securities Lending and Borrowing Program was launched to facilitate timely settlement and improve market liquidity. This program anticipated the recommendation of the Group of Thirty, a leading international financial industry association, that securities lending and borrowing be made readily available. It was substantially automated in 1983. In 1991, securities lending and borrowing was integrated into the Euroclear Securities Settlement Processing.

In 1980 settlement of transactions between counterparties in the Euroclear System and Cedel was automated by an electronic link, known as the 'bridge'. This link has allowed the international securities markets to expand by minimising clearance and settlement delays and costs whilst preserving a competitive choice of clearance systems for market participants. Similarly, links with other clearance systems, both long-standing such as with Deutscher Auslandskassenverein AG in Germany and those more recently established such as with SICOVAM, Banque de France and Reserve Bank of New Zealand provide for more efficient exchanges with those markets.

Since the mid-1980s, the range of securities accepted for clearance and settlement in the Euroclear System has been extended from Eurobonds to include many other types of securities, including foreign and domestic debt securities, money market instruments such as commercial paper, warrants and convertible debt issues. Since April 1986, the Euroclear System has included clearance and settlement services tailored for internationally-traded equities.

For the market, the Euroclear System's success is measured by its growing volumes. The value of securities held on behalf of participants was $1.12

trillion at the end of 1991. Transactions settled were valued at approximately $5.74 trillion in 1991, with daily instruction volume averaging over 30,000 and peaks exceeding 40,000. Average daily securities loans outstanding were $2.8 billion in 1991.

All participants have the opportunity to own shares in Euroclear Clearance System Société Coopérative (the 'Cooperative'), a Belgian cooperative corporation and more than 2200 are now members and participate in decision making. The Board of Directors of the cooperative represents the interests of all participants. It decides policy for the Euroclear System, including fees and rebates, categories of securities accepted, approval of depositaries and admission of new participants. The Euroclear System is operated under contract by Morgan Guaranty Trust Company of New York, at its Euroclear Operations Centre (EOC) in Brussels.

Through this single central access point, participants in the Euroclear System are able to use four basic services: (1) multicurrency securities clearance and settlement, (2) securities lending and borrowing, (3) custody and (4) money transfer.

The Euroclear System: Securities Clearance and Settlement

Before considering the core settlement process, it is important to understand the daily processing cycle at EOC and the matching of trade information.

Participants purchasing securities send to EOC instructions to receive securities and sellers send instructions to deliver. Instructions are validated automatically for processing. Invalid instructions are rejected. The computerised process attempts to match a participant's valid instruction to receive with the counterparty's instruction to deliver. The objective is to ensure that the terms of the trade are identical in the two instructions. Matching is continuous through the day as valid instructions are received. Information required for matching includes: (1) account numbers of the two parties, (2) settlement date, (3) quantity of securities, (4) the security code of the issue traded, and (5) currency and cash countervalue. Valid but unmatched instructions are recycled through the matching process until they are either matched or cancelled.

EOC takes matched instructions for a given settlement date together with any instructions remaining unsettled from previous days and passes them into the next step, settlement.

The Securities Settlement Processing
The Euroclear Securities Settlement Processing takes place during the night prior to the scheduled settlement date. A matched instruction having reached

its settlement date settles if the seller has sufficient securities in its account and the buyer has adequate cash or credit.

Cash and securities positions resulting from the overnight settlement processing are reported to participants in the early morning (Brussels time), at the end of the settlement processing cycle. For the beginning of each business day, EOC reports to each participant which of its securities transactions settled and which did not, and the resulting cash and securities positions. An important advantage of overnight processing prior to settlement date is that by reporting early on settlement date it gives participants effective same-day cash management capabilities.

In the Euroclear System, there is no separate cash payment cycle and, in part because the risks associated with a separate payment cycle are absent, there is no netting of transactions. Rather, simultaneous book-entry movements of cash and securities are made as a result of using a transaction-by-transaction procedure that recycles cash and securities shown to be received during the securities settlement processing cycle. Thus, cash and securities resulting from one transaction can be used to settle another in the same processing cycle. This procedure enables a participant to settle the maximum possible number of transactions with the resources available. In addition, it allows participants considerable flexibility as they may assign settlement priorities to specific transactions.

Interest, dividends and redemption proceeds are also made available during the Securities Settlement Processing. Payments are generally credited on the interest, dividend or redemption payment date.

For settlement with the system, the value date of cash debits and credits is generally the value date of processing (or the date of closing for new issues). Settlements that require deliveries to or receipts from local markets generally have the date of local payment as cash value date.

Securities are credited as soon as settlement within the system is final; securities received from outside the Euroclear System are credited in accordance with procedures which vary with the different types of receipts.

A participant with transactions that fail to settle because there are insufficient securities in its Securities Clearance Account may borrow the necessary securities using the Euroclear Securities Lending and Borrowing Program either (i) automatically or (ii) by sending specific requests to EOC.

The Euroclear System: Securities Lending and Borrowing

The Euroclear Securities Lending and Borrowing Program was designed in 1975 to improve the efficiency of securities settlement and increase market liquidity. Since 1975 the program has been improved continuously. What began as a manual process was automated as a pre-settlement procedure in

1983. In 1991 it became a dynamic process within the Securities Settlement Processing.

The Euroclear Securities Lending and Borrowing Program allows participants holding stable portfolios of securities to increase overall yield (without loss of ownership benefits) by lending securities to other participants which seek to avoid failed settlements because of lack of securities.

Borrowers in the program are usually active traders such as market-makers or dealers. Participants may be either automatic borrowers, providing standing instructions to EOC both to identify and, if possible, meet their borrowing needs following the established procedures of the program, or opportunity borrowers, retaining the responsibility for submitting their own borrowing requests. Borrowings are reimbursed automatically as soon as sufficient securities are available in the account of the borrower. All borrowers can choose the categories of securities, currencies and specific issues which they wish to borrow.

Lenders in the program are mainly portfolio managers and custodians who are not active traders. These participants may become either automatic lenders or opportunity lenders. Automatic lenders provide standing instructions to EOC to lend certain portions of their portfolios when opportunities arise and authorise EOC to determine the securities available for lending under established procedures. Lenders may also exclude certain securities, types of instruments or currencies. Opportunity lenders are asked by EOC to lend securities whenever the supply of securities from automatic lenders appears inadequate to meet all borrowing needs.

To ensure liquidity in the market, aggregate borrowings are limited to specified percentages of each outstanding issue (by issue and by borrower). The percentage varies depending on the trading characteristics of each particular type of issue.

Lenders are credited automatically with the amount of any interest or dividends as if they still held such securities and they may recall a loan at any time. Lenders also retain the collateral value of loaned securities to secure their own borrowings through the system.

EOC provides participants with comprehensive reports about their lending and borrowing activity. Reports are available through EUCLID (the Euroclear System's proprietary communications structure), telex and mail.

Morgan Guaranty Brussels guarantees the return of loaned securities and distributions on loaned securities (or the cash equivalent if the securities cannot be obtained) if a borrower fails to return the securities.

The Euroclear System: Custody

Euroclear participants have access to extensive custody-related services including safekeeping, collection of interest, dividend and redemption payments, advance notice of deadlines and corporate events affecting their securities, assistance with tax certification and recovery and assistance with custody operations such as exercise of warrants, conversions and other options or corporate actions.

The operation of the Euroclear System is designed to minimise the need to move physical securities. Securities are immobilised in the Euroclear depositary network, which includes major depositary banks, national clearance systems and central banks in many countries around the world. Securities held in the network are managed centrally by EOC, including the effecting and monitoring of external receipts and deliveries of securities.

Securities accepted in the Euroclear System are assigned to and held by the most conveniently located depositary (specialised depositary). Once deposited into the system, all securities of an issue are held on a fungible basis. Most deposits are made with the relevant specialised depositary and therefore processed very quickly.

Most securities may be deposited only at the specialised depositary for the issue which checks the security. Certain securities may also be deposited at other depositaries, but are frozen until realigned to and checked by the specialised depositary. Rules and clear procedures for deposits are designed to protect the system and its participants.

Virtually all new issues of internationally-traded securities including euro-commercial paper and many important international equity offerings are closed and distributed on a same-day against payment basis through the international clearance systems. Centralised distribution of securities against payment facilitates control of allotment payments from participants to the Lead Manager. The majority of primary distributions of securities issued in the Euro-markets are distributed through the Euroclear System. Assistance is also provided with the administration of the exchange of global certificates for definitive certificates.

The Euroclear System: Money Transfer

In order to support their securities settlement processing, participants have a cash account with Morgan Guaranty, Brussels. This cash account consists of a sub-division for each of the currencies and composite currencies accepted in the Euroclear System.

The cash account is used primarily for settlement of securities transactions, payments for new issue distributions and receipt of income and redemption proceeds. In addition, participants' cash accounts may be used for book transfers of funds between participants, wire transfers for payment of funds out of the system, credits of funds received into the system, foreign exchange conversions and operations resulting from the aggregation or disaggregation of Special Drawing Rights. Participants may also preadvise funds to be received.

Participants are able to use S.W.I.F.T, telex, or mail to send their money transfer instructions.

The EUCLID Telecommunications Structure

Most Euroclear participants use EUCLID, a proprietary telecommunications structure that provides efficient, secure and reliable input and execution reporting functions for participant instructions. The EUCLID system was introduced in 1979 and has been progressively developed ever since. It has been substantially improved and relaunched as EUCLID 90, the communication system for the nineties. By introducing local data entry and computer-to-computer communication, EUCLID reduced the cost and increased the efficiency of communicating settlement instructions worldwide. EUCLID provides comprehensive input of trade and settlement data for confirmation, as well as reporting of matching results and settlement information, as well as information about custody, securities lending and borrowing, and advance notices of events affecting securities participants hold in the system.

Participants may also communicate with EOC by S.W.I.F.T, telex, or mail.

5: The Taxation of International Lending Transactions

Jürgen Jung, Arthur Andersen & Co. G.m.b.H, Frankfurt

The description following is a general guideline in order to obtain an overview of the taxation of securities lending transactions in various countries. Before the initiation of any specific transactions, further detailed expertise should be requested from competent consultants. This overview has been compiled by our Frankfurt office under the guidance of Jürgen Jung with the support of our offices in London, New York, Paris and Tokyo. It complies with the status of tax regulations as of August 1991.

The following persons have contributed the country sections:

Frankfurt: Jürgen Jung, Rosheen Quraishi, Claudia Nik; London: Kathy Kock, Liz Giles; Paris: Claire Acard, Delphine Nougayrede; New York: Gerald Maugieri, Carmela Reiman; Tokyo: Eiki Kawakami, Shigeru Nonaka.

1. INTRODUCTION

1.1. Types of Securities Lending Transactions

Securities lending generally comprises the following transactions:

(a) The lending of securities against a commission fee payment. This kind of securities lending is undertaken in order to overcome short-term bottlenecks in the delivery of securities for the fulfilment of certain transactions.

   Furthermore securities lending is used for short-sale transactions, i.e., for the sale of stocks which are currently not at the disposal of the seller. In order to fulfil the obligation to deliver the securities from such a short-sale, the seller borrows securities and purchases securities later on in order to retransfer them to the lender.

(b) Repurchase (buy and sell) transactions performed such that either securities are bought/sold with a predefined forward reverse transaction or that the buyer has the right but not the obligation to retransfer the underlying securities to the seller.

Nevertheless, not all types of securities lending transactions are common in every country. The chapters describing securities lending transactions in the various countries depict the characteristics of the respective types of transactions prevalent in each country.

1.2. General Aspects of the Taxation of Securities Lending Transactions

In some countries the tax treatment of securities lending transactions corresponds to and follows the accounting treatment of the transaction. Therefore for such cases a brief description of the accounting treatment is necessary to facilitate the better understanding of the tax treatment. For this purpose in the following a short caption on the accounting method precedes the tax treatment in the respective relevant cases.

For accounting purposes due to the fact that the accounting treatment for securities usually depends on the economic ownership, it is important to determine whether the legal and economic ownership of the securities remain with the lender or are passed on to the borrower.

A profit realisation can take place upon the transfer of the securities (i.e. in the case that the securities are transferred at market values higher than book values).

The tax treatment of securities lending transactions includes the allocation of income derived from the securities (interest and dividend payments) to the lender or the borrower and the income tax treatment of the compensation payments made during the term of the lending transaction (dividend and interest payments that the borrower has to pass on to the lender; for private as well as for business investors). In connection with the income derived from the securities, possible tax credits may arise due to taxes being withheld at source. Furthermore, net asset taxes or transfer taxes may become applicable.

2. TAX TREATMENT OF SECURITIES LENDING TRANSACTIONS IN GERMANY

2.1. Securities Lending Transactions as described under 1.1(a)

Such securities lending transactions are executed via the Deutscher Kassenverein (DKV) on the one hand and by Commercial Banks on the other, as described in Part I, Chapter 2.

Accounting Treatment

At present, no specific accounting regulations for this type of securities lending transactions exist. Therefore, the accounting has to follow the generally accepted accounting principles. The businessman has to disclose all his assets and liabilities in the balance sheet.

As the *borrower* acquires the legal as well as the economic ownership of the securities – he is not restricted in the disposal of the securities and only has the obligation to retransfer similar securities back to the lender – he has to disclose the securities in his balance sheet at market value. At the same time he has to show a liability against the lender in the same amount.

The *lender*, on the other hand, reduces his balance sheet position 'Securities' by the book value of the securities and capitalises a receivable against the borrower in the amount of the securities' book value.

Income Tax Treatment

By means of the lending transaction itself, no *profit realisation* occurs for the lender as he transfers the securities to the borrower at the securities' book value and books a receivable in the same amount. The claim against the lender only represents an equivalent for the transferred securities. This tax treatment has been confirmed by a release of the German tax authorities.

The balance sheet effect for the borrower is only an increase in assets and liabilities, both in the amount of the market value of the securities.

During the term of the lending transaction all *interest and dividend payments* derived from the securities are attributed to the borrower being both the economic and legal owner of the securities. These payments qualify either as income from business (§15 German Income Tax Law; business property) or as income from capital investments (German Income Tax Law; private property).

In order to compensate the lender for the lost income the borrower will have to make a payment to the lender corresponding to the equivalent of the interest/dividend payments derived from the securities including potential tax credits (compensation payment). Furthermore, the borrower has to pay a commission fee for the securities lending transaction itself.

In the case that the securities are part of the business assets the payments to the lender will be taxable as income from business (§15 German Income Tax Law) for the lender and deductible as business expenses for the borrower on an accrued basis.

A private lender realises income from other sources (§22 No. 3 German Income Tax Law) whereas a private borrower can deduct the compensation payments as expenses connected directly to the income as long as there is no disproportion between the income from the securities and the expenses of the lending transaction.

For German tax purposes the criteria of legal ownership determines the right to claim income resulting from investments in securities. This includes the dividend or interest payments as well as any underlying *tax credits*. As a consequence, the borrower of the securities can claim the underlying tax credit for dividend payments (disregarding any cases that would fall under the 'substance over form' category).

For *net asset tax* purposes, the borrower has to disclose the received securities as an asset position in the schedule of property whereas the respective liability forms a liability position.

The lender has to assess the receivable against the borrower with the market value of the securities. The securities are eliminated from the schedule of property for the term of the lending transaction.

According to §4 No. 8e *Value Added Tax* (VAT) Law, securities lending transactions are tax exempt from VAT. In addition, the *Stock Exchange Turnover Tax* has been abolished as from 1 January 1991 onwards. Therefore, no transfer taxes accrue on securities lending transactions in Germany.

2.2. Repurchase Transactions

As described in Part I, Chapter 2, other types of securities lending transactions in Germany are the so-called 'repo transactions' (*Pensionsgeschäfte*). One kind of repo transaction, 'Echte Pensionsgeschäfte', entails the obligation for the purchaser to retransfer the same securities to the seller at a later date. On the other hand 'Unechte Pensionsgeschäfte' give the right, but not the obligation to the purchaser to return the securities to the seller.

The accounting principles for 'Pensionsgeschäfte' are laid down in §340b German Commercial Code as of 1 January 1991 and become applicable from 1993 onwards. Although §340b German Commercial Code is generally obligatory for banks, this accounting rule will be applicable for other companies as well.

The *accounting treatment* for 'Unechte Pensionsgeschäfte' as defined above is as follows (§340b para. 5 German Commercial Code): The securities have to be disclosed in the balance sheet of the purchaser, who acquires the legal and economic ownership, whereas the seller has to show the price agreed upon for the repurchase of the securities in a note below the balance sheet.

The accounting treatment for 'Echte Pensionsgeschäfte' (§340b para. 4 German Commercial Code) is as follows: The purchaser becomes the legal but not the economic owner of the securities, therefore the securities are attributed to the seller for accounting purposes so that they remain in his balance sheet without any changes. The seller has to set up a liability against the purchaser in the received cash amount. In the case that the amount agreed upon for the retransfer of the securities is lower or higher than the amount received at the beginning, the difference has to be spread over the term of the repurchase transaction. The purchaser shows a receivable in his balance sheet for the amount paid to the seller. He also has to disclose a possible difference between the purchase and the sales price.

The income (dividend or interest income from the securities) is attributed in the same manner as in the above described transactions either to the purchaser or the seller as only the legal owner of the securities has the right to claim income from securities. As a consequence, the *tax treatment* does not differ from the one already described. The economic ownership does not have any influence on the attribution of the securities' income for tax purposes to either the seller or the purchaser. It is of no importance which party discloses the securities in the balance sheet.

3. TAX TREATMENT OF SECURITIES LENDING TRANSACTIONS IN FRANCE

Securities lending techniques available on the French market can be broken down into three main categories: securities lending transactions, 'remere' sales and newly developed pensions with delivery (*pensions livrées*).

From a tax standpoint, the only clearly defined rules are those set down in the law No. 87–416 dated 17 June 1987, the subsequent laws (law No. 88–1201 dated 23 December 1988 and law No. 91–716 dated 26 July 1991) governing certain lending transactions. Conversely, securities remeres and pensions with delivery have not yet been legally regulated taxwise by the authorities.

3.1. Securities Lending Transactions

A number of legal, tax and accounting rules applicable to securities lending transactions were set down in the above mentioned law of 1987 subsequently modified. Lending operations can nevertheless be carried out outside of the legal framework: the law only governs those transactions meeting specific requirements, amongst which the requirement that a dividend period or a coupon period with an attached tax credit should *not* be crossed in the lending transaction, and that the transaction should not last more than one year must be fulfilled.

When the legal requirements are not met in a transaction, the tax rules laid down in the law of 1987 are not applicable: the transaction then conveys fiscal uncertainty to a certain extent. The contents of the law set out below should therefore be considered as describing the general taxation pattern of most qualifying securities lending transactions. Given that the accounting treatment of qualifying lending transactions is in general in line with their corporate tax treatment, both are simultaneously addressed below. Nevertheless, securities lending transactions pledged by cash and entered into by French banks should be treated, from an accounting point of view, as pensions with delivery.

Tax Treatment

The main feature of the tax treatment of qualifying securities lending is the non-recognition of capital gains or losses although legal ownership of the securities is transferred to the borrower (in some instances, however, gains or losses will have to be recognised depending on the nature of the securities; this is particularly the case when lending securities which are drawn from a bank trading portfolio).

Upon implementation of the transaction and transfer of the securities to the borrower, the securities are replaced on the balance sheet of the *lender* by a separate receivable registered at the historical value of the securities. Accordingly, no *capital gain or loss* is recognised for accounting and tax purposes. Similarly, loss provisions previously booked are not added back to the taxable result of the year.

During the period covered by the transaction, the corresponding receivable should, from an accounting point of view, be valuated at year end according to the nature of the securities lent. For tax purposes, losses resulting from such a valuation at year end, if any, are not deductible from the taxable result (except in the case where securities lent have been drawn from a bank trading portfolio).

Upon termination of the transaction, the returned securities are registered on the balance sheet at the value of the receivable, i.e. at the historical value of the securities. Accordingly, no capital gain or loss is recognised for accounting and tax purposes.

If the returned securities are subsequently sold or transferred by the lender, their date of acquisition for determining the applicable rate of capital gains tax (reduced rates for certain kind of securities held for more than two years, normal rates in the other case) will be considered that of initial acquisition irrespective of the lending transaction.

A major exception to the above rules is when the lender is a bank and the securities loaned are drawn from the bank's trading portfolio. Such securities are indeed subject to mark-to-market assessment at year end for accounting and tax purposes. Under this assumption, gains or losses must be recognised upon implementation and termination of the transaction and the receivable is valuated at year end according to mark-to-market rules.

Upon implementation of the transaction and transfer of the securities to the *borrower*, the securities are booked on the balance sheet of the borrower at their market value. Conversely the obligation to return the securities upon termination of the transaction is represented by a corresponding payable. Accordingly, no *profit or loss* is recognised for accounting and tax purposes.

At year end both the securities and the payable are valued according to the market value of the securities. The impact on the profit and loss statement therefore remains neutral.

Eventually, upon termination of the lending transaction, the securities are deemed returned at the book value of the corresponding payable. No capital gain or loss is recognised.

The only instance where a profit or loss will occur is when the borrowed securities are sold by the borrower and then bought back before termination.

No *interest or dividend payments* giving rise to a tax credit can occur in a qualifying lending transaction. Interest and dividends without any tax credit are paid to the borrower and taxed at his level, as a result of the legal transfer of ownership to the borrower.

Commission fees paid to the lender by the borrower cannot be less than interest or dividend payments made during the period covered by the transaction, if any. The net fee is taxable on an accrued basis.

Under the provisions of the law of 1987, commission fees made to the lender by the borrower are *VAT* exempt, and securities lending transactions should be exempt from *stamp duties*.

3.2. Remere Transactions

From a legal standpoint, remere transactions are governed by civil law provisions under which they are defined as sales where the seller has an option to cancel the transaction within a five year period. In practice, the option is usually always exercised at much shorter notice.

Securities remere transactions as such are not officially regulated from a tax perspective. Therefore they are characterised by fiscal uncertainty enhanced by the difference between their legal nature and their accounting treatment.

Accounting Treatment
Further to accounting regulations introduced in 1989, the accounting treatment of remere transactions mirrors more their economic nature (i.e., financial loans pledged by securities) than their legal definition (i.e., sales with an option to cancel).

Upon sale of the securities, the *seller* recognises a *capital gain or loss* in its profit and loss statement. However, if it appears highly likely that the option to cancel the sale will be exercised, which is generally the case, the capital gain or loss is eliminated at year end. Therefore, in practice, no profit or loss is recognised ('economic treatment').

Moreover, valuation at year end and accrued interest are taken into account as if the securities had remained on the balance sheet. The compensation payment that will be made to the purchaser is also booked *prorata temporis*.

Upon exercise of the option, the securities are registered on the balance sheet at their historical value as a result of the cancellation of the sale. All balance sheet recordings in relation to the remere sale are reversed. In the case where the initial gain or loss has not been eliminated at year end, it is cancelled at the time the option is exercised.

Upon purchase of the securities, the *purchaser* books them at their purchase price on the balance sheet. If it appears highly likely that the option will be exercised by the seller, which is usually the case, the compensation payment is booked *prorata temporis* as income. The securities are not revalued at year end.

Upon exercise of the option, the balance sheet recordings in relation to the remere purchase are reversed and annulled. No *capital gain or loss* is therefore recognised.

Tax Treatment

The analysis set forth below relates to the case where the exercise of the option is highly probable at year end since it is the most frequent situation encountered in practice. In such a situation, the accounting treatment should follow the economic reality.

The *seller* must basically choose between a tax treatment in line with the economic situation and the accounting treatment (i.e., neutrality when the exercise of the option appears likely), or a tax treatment based on the legal nature of the transaction (i.e., recognition of the capital gain or loss and annulment at the exercise of the option).

When the first approach is adopted, no tax deductions or add-backs are necessary. When the second approach is adopted, however, fiscal adjustments have to be made which are reversed upon exercise of the option: add-backs or deductions of capital gains in respect of remeres outstanding at year end as well as of booked unrealised losses, if any.

The purchase is treated as an ordinary asset purchase. However, no unrealised loss can be recognised at year end with respect to the securities due to the absence of corresponding book recordings. Upon exercise of the option, the balance sheet recordings are reversed.

Before the exercise of the option, *interest or dividend payments* in respect of the sold securities are made to the purchaser, as a result of the transfer of ownership. The situation as regards attached tax credits is debatable. The parties can decide to transfer back such payments to the seller by means of decreasing the commission fee.

The *commission fee* can be considered either as interest taxable or deductible on an accrued basis (economic analysis), or as an ordinary income/expense taxable or deductible only when actually paid out (legal analysis). In the second alternative, fiscal adjustments at year end are necessary.

Commission fees are *VAT* exempt. Remere contracts could be subject to *registration duties* depending on the nature of the securities dealt. Nevertheless, they should not be subject to the special tax on securities transactions (*impôt de bourse*).

3.3. Pension with Delivery

Pension with delivery entails the transfer of a given amount of securities versus cash payment over a given period. Upon termination, the transaction is reversed and the seller must buy back the securities. As compensation, the purchaser is paid a fee by the seller.

The legal status of pensions with delivery is not settled by the law and the legal qualification of the transaction is still uncertain. The transactions are nevertheless governed by a market convention applicable from 1 July 1990. Under the convention, the purchaser has legal ownership of the securities during the period covered by the transaction.

Accounting Treatment
The accounting treatment of pensions has been defined for banks only.

Upon transfer, the securities remain on the balance sheet of the *seller*. The transfer of cash gives rise to a corresponding payable. At year end, both the securities and the payables are valuated according to usual accounting rules. Upon termination, all entries in relation to the pension are reversed. No capital gain or loss is therefore recognised.

The *purchaser* books a receivable on his balance sheet. The securities as such are not recorded. The receivable is valuated at year end according to usual accounting rules. Upon termination, the entries are reversed. No capital gain or loss is therefore recognised.

All *interest and dividend payments* with respect to the securities, as well as any attached tax credits, are made to the purchaser due to the transfer of ownership. The *commission fee* received (paid) in respect of the transaction is recognised by the purchaser (seller) on a *prorata temporis* basis.

Tax Treatment
Regarding *corporate tax*, two letters were issued by the authorities in 1990 and 1991 mentioning that pensions with delivery would be treated as tax neutral where the market convention is abided by. However, these letters have not been confirmed yet by official provisions.

Regarding other taxes, remuneration payments are *VAT* exempt and it is unclear whether other indirect taxes are applicable.

4. TAX TREATMENT OF SECURITIES LENDING TRANSACTIONS IN JAPAN

4.1. Securities Lending Transactions

The lending of securities against a commission fee payment is comprised of two types: the pure lending type and the finance type. In the case of the pure lending type, the borrower must return the identical securities; in the case of the finance type, the borrower must not return the identical securities, but is able to close the transaction by the delivery of the same brand of the securities. A transaction can be structured as either type in accordance with the wishes and agreements of the parties of the transaction.

Tax Treatment for Pure Lending Type Transactions
The legal and economic ownership will be retained by the lender. This amount remains tax exempt. In the case of income tax being withheld on dividends or interest payments, the lender can claim the underlying *tax credit*.

In a pure lending type transaction no *profit realisation* will take place.

Tax Treatment for Finance Type Transactions
In contrast to pure lending type transactions, the legal and economic ownership in finance type transactions is transferred to the borrower. He is entitled to claim *tax credits* for income tax withheld on dividends or interest payments.

In a finance type transaction no *profit realisation* occurs.

On both types of securities lending transactions neither income tax on commission fee payments nor a *securities transaction tax* will be levied.

In case the securities lending is used for *short-sale transactions*, a profit will not be realised until delivery of securities or until the short-sale transaction is closed otherwise by entering into a short-purchase transaction.

4.2. Repurchase Agreements

According to a notification of the Ministry of Finance (MOF) in connection with the repurchase transactions dated 10 March 1976, the following requirements are necessary for repurchase agreements:

- Listed corporations and any other corporations, whose financial con-

ditions are comparable to those of listed corporations, are able to enter into repurchase transactions.
- Only government bonds and corporate bonds can be traded in repurchase agreements, stocks are not tradable for such transactions.
- A trade price is limited within a certain statutory range and the term of the transaction is limited to one year at the most. A securities company which deals with these transactions must report the status monthly to the MOF.

Tax Treatment
For tax purposes, repurchase transactions are basically treated as a loan. However, for tax purposes it is also possible to treat such a transaction as a buy-and-sale of securities provided that such a treatment is applied consistently.

In the case where repurchase transactions are treated as a *loan* for tax purposes, the coupon interest paid on securities during the term of the transaction will be considered as income for the seller. The seller may deduct or credit the withholding income tax for the whole period the borrower holds the securities.

If repurchase transactions are treated as a *buy-and-sale of securities* for tax purposes, any *interest payments* on the securities during the term of the transaction will be attributed to the buyer. The seller may not deduct or credit the withholding income tax whereas the buyer is entitled to deduct or credit it for the period from the beginning of this transaction to the interest payment date.

On repurchase agreements a *securities transaction tax* is levied.

5. ACCOUNTING AND TAX TREATMENT OF SECURITIES LENDING TRANSACTIONS IN THE UK

5.1. Securities Lending Transactions

Accounting Treatment
The securities are not shown on the balance sheet of the *borrower* but should be disclosed as a financial commitment in the notes to the accounts.

The securities remain on the balance sheet of the *lender* and the normal accounting policy of the lending company in relation to securities, e.g. the mark to market principle should be applied.

If *commission fees* are paid (or received) on the deal, there is an argument to recognise this upfront payment (or receipt) in the profit and loss account. However, the arrangement fee is usually indistinguishable from the lump sum paid (or received) on the deal. Therefore, it would only be appropriate and prudent to amortise the whole cost (or fee receivable) to the profit and loss account over the term of the securities lending transaction.

Tax Treatment

For *corporation income tax* purposes any separately identifiable fees and commissions will be taxable for the lender (and deductible for the borrower) immediately. If certain conditions are met the transaction will not constitute a disposal for tax purposes. The main conditions are that the borrower is a recognised market maker, the transaction takes place through a money broker and all lenders are approved by the Inland Revenue. If these conditions are met, the lender will still be subject to tax on the interest and dividend payments from the securities as if the transaction had not occurred.

It is important to note that if the qualifying conditions are not met very complicated tax consequences arise in the UK particularly in the treatment of 'manufactured payments'. These are payments made by the borrower to compensate the lender for not receiving the dividends or interest which would have been received had the securities not been transferred.

For *withholding tax* purposes a basic rate of currently 25 per cent will be withheld at source from interest payments. This may be offset against the recipient's liability to withhold income tax on any interest payments made or against any corporation tax liability.

A UK company must account for advance corporation tax (ACT) of $33\frac{1}{3}$ per cent on any dividend payment. This may be offset against its corporation tax liability to a maximum of 25 per cent of taxable profits, or against the recipient company's own liability to account for this tax on its own dividends.

Moreover, securities lending transactions are exempt from *UK value added tax* (VAT) if the transaction is concluded with a person within the UK or EC. If the counterparty is outside the EC the transaction will not be exempt but the rate of VAT will be 0 per cent.

5.2. Repurchase Agreements

Accounting Treatment

The *purchaser* of the securities will treat the deal as a secured lending of cash. Therefore, the securities will be shown under receivables and the mark to market principle will not apply. Moreover, the entire benefit of the purchase/sale should be amortised to the profit and loss account over the term of the loan. This cost would include the profit and loss on the purchase/sale and any coupon accruals for the term of the loan.

The *seller* of the securities will treat the deal as a secured borrowing of cash. Therefore, the securities remain on the balance sheet and the normal accounting policy of the company, e.g. mark to market principle applies to the position. The entire cost of the sale/purchase should be amortised to the profit and loss account over the term of the loan. A payable is recognised on the balance sheet in the amount of the borrowed cash.

If the purchaser has an option to retransfer the securities, the accounting treatment will depend on the likelihood of the option being exercised. If the pricing of the option makes exercise likely, it may be treated as for a repurchase agreement. Otherwise, it will be treated as a sale by the seller with a contingent liability shown in the accounts.

Tax Treatment
Special provisions applicable to securities lending transactions (see 5.1 above) will still apply provided that the purchaser has borrowed in order to fulfil a sale contract on the securities.

However, if there is no obligation for the purchaser to retransfer the securities, these provisions will not apply. In this situation the seller will be subject to tax on any *capital gains* arising on the transfer. The purchaser will also be subject to tax on any capital gains if the securities are transferred back to the seller.

6. TAX TREATMENT OF SECURITIES LENDING TRANSACTIONS IN THE UNITED STATES

6.1. Securities Lending Transactions

Section 1058 of the Internal Revenue Code provides for the non-recognition of *capital gains or losses* to the taxpayer on the exchange of securities for an obligation pursuant to an agreement which meets certain requirements. To qualify for non-recognition of capital gains or losses, the agreement must:

— provide for the return to the lender of securities identical to the securities loaned:
— require that payments being made to the lender have to be equal to the interest, dividend and other payments to which the owner of the securities is entitled during the period of the loan (compensation payments);
— ensure that the lender bears the total risk of loss or opportunity for gain in the securities loaned;
— meet any other requirements prescribed by Regulations.

Proposed regulations require that the agreement has to be in writing and must allow the lender to terminate the loan on notice of not more than five business days.

The lender's tax basis of the contractual obligation is the same as the tax basis of the securities loaned. When the identical securities are returned to the lender, the tax basis carries over to the returned securities. The lender's holding period for the obligation includes the period he held the exchanged securities and subsequently tacks on to the holding period of the returned securities.

In transactions collateralised by cash, a percentage of the return is paid to the securities lender as a *commission fee*. In the case of loans collateralised by other securities, a predetermined fee is used. The regulations do not address the characterisation of commission fees.

All amounts paid by a borrower to a lender in respect of *interest, dividends or other payments* made on loaned securities during the term of the loan, are characterised as fees for the temporary use of securities. Therefore, a corporate lender will not qualify for the dividends received deduction with respect to compensation payments reflecting dividends. This rule serves to prevent a duplication of favourable tax attributes associated with distributions on a particular security.

6.2. Repurchase Transactions

Generally, repurchase agreements are characterised as *secured loans* and accordingly, no capital gain or loss on the sale of securities will be recognised. On the other hand, a repo may be treated as an actual *sale* depending on the substance of the transaction. In determining whether a repo should be treated as a sale the following factors should be considered:

- whether the obligation to repurchase the securities at some specified date is in writing;
- the intent of the parties;
- whether the buyer collects income derived from the securities as its own;
- whether the seller pays any interest on the funds;
- whether the seller is required to repurchase the securities;
- whether the buyer can resell the securities and keep the profits as its own.

Transactions Treated as a Sale of Securities
If a repo is deemed to be a sale, the seller recognises a *gain or loss* on the transfer of the securities. The buyer's tax basis is equal to the purchase price, and the holding period starts on the purchase date. Any *interest or dividend payments* derived from the securities will be recognised by the buyer, the owner of the securities. Upon the repurchase of the securities, the same tax effects occur, i.e., the buyer is treated as having sold the securities.

Transactions Treated as Secured Loans

Although they may be structured differently, securities loan transactions and repurchase agreements treated as secured loans are similar in many respects. In both transactions, the beneficial owner of the securities retains the economic benefits and burdens of ownership. In addition, in both transactions, the lender receives a fee for a secured loan of property. In a repurchase agreement, cash is being loaned with securities serving as collateral whereas in a securities loan, cash or other property are used as collateral for the borrowed securities.

In a repo transaction treated as a secured loan, the repurchase margin paid by the seller on repurchasing the securities is deemed to be interest. Any *interest or dividends* derived from the securities during the term of the loan must be remitted to the seller. The character of such payments to the seller is unclear.

Index

ACT, see advance corporation tax
advance corporation tax (ACT) 151
against payment settlement 132, 133
agent bank 114
agent de change 47, 50
Allianz 33, 38
arbitrage 10, 12, 13, 39, 49, 54, 55, 59, 63, 64, 65, 72, 81, 90, 128
Association of German Banks 20
assured payment 13, 14, 15, 19, 116
automatic borrower 125, 126, 128, 137
automatic lender 31, 32, 125, 126, 128, 130, 137
avoir fiscal 56, 64

Bank of England 10, 12, 14, 15, 16, 127
Bank of Tokyo 37
Bankruptcy Amendment 1984 93
Bankruptcy Code 1978 93
Banque Bruxelles Lambert SA 127
Banque de France 53, 58, 61, 134
Banque Générale du Luxembourg 127
Banque Indosuez 47, 63
Banque Internationale à Luxembourg 127
Banque Paribas 63
basis trading 88
BBL Intermediation 63
Beaudoin 50
Bevill, Bresler and Schulman 91
BHF Bank 37
Big Bang 9
Black Monday 67, 71
BNP 63
Bobls, see Bundesobligationen
British government stock 15
broker dealer 1, 2, 3, 4, 5, 6, 24, 37, 96, 132, 133
Buisson 50
Bulldog bonds 15
Bundesaufsichtsamt, see Federal Banking Supervisory Office
Bundesbank 24, 34, 39, 42, 43, 100
Bundesobligationen (Bobls) 26, 33, 38

Bundesschatzanweisungen 33
Bundesverband der deutschen Banken 20
Bunds (Bundesanleihen) 20, 21, 23, 26, 27, 33, 38, 100, 101
buy/sellback repo 39

CAC40 63
capital adequacy 95
Capital Gains Tax 18, 145, 152
capital gains tax (France) 47, 57, 59, 61
capital requirements 95
Capital Transaction Tax Law, Article 22 26
Cascade system 31
case-by-case borrower 125, 126
case-by-case lender 125, 126
cash collateral (Germany) 34, 42, 43
cash collateral (Japan) 76, 77
cash settlement market (France) 48
CCF 63
CDs, see certificates of deposit
Cedel 31, 37, 102, 124, 125, 126, 127, 128, 133
Central Gilts Office (CGO) 12, 13, 15, 16, 19
Central Moneymarkets Office 15, 16
Centrale de Livraison de Valeurs Mobiliers SA, see Cedel
certificates of deposit 5, 14, 73, 93
CGO, see Central Gilts Office
CHAPS 12
cheap money 14, 17
Cheuvreux de Virieu 63
Citibank NA 126
Clifford Chance 107
CMO, see Central Moneymarkets Office
COB, see Commission des Opérations de Bourse
collateral 3, 4, 5, 14, 15, 17, 18, 32, 33, 36, 38, 59, 61, 62, 64, 81, 82, 83, 84, 102, 107, 109, 110, 111, 112, 113, 127, 129, 137
collateral, general 83, 84, 96

155

collateral (Japan) 73, 74, 76
collateral, special issue 83, 86, 87
collateral, stock 83
commercial paper 134
Commission des Opérations de Bourse 50
Compagnie Parisienne de Reescompte 63
contango (marché des reports) 49, 54, 59, 61
convertible bonds 2, 65
convertible bonds (Japan) 71
convertible debt issues 134
convertibles 16, 127, 134
corporate tax (France) 56, 145, 148
Corporation and Commonwealth stock 15
corporation tax 18, 151
Cotinter 63
counterparty risk 3, 109, 110, 132
coupon 57, 98, 114, 144, 151
coupon payment 83, 92
Crédit Commercial de France 127
credit risk 108, 109, 110, 115, 126
credit risk (France) 60
currency options 116
custodian 3, 53, 54, 74, 85, 102, 107, 108, 114, 119, 120, 122, 132
custody 26, 29, 75, 129, 131, 135, 138
custody transfer (Japan) 70, 71

DAC-RAP, see delivery against cash-receipt against payment
Daily Official List 17
DAX, see Deutsche Aktien Index
daylight exposure 5, 19, 113
dear money 14, 17
delivery against cash-receipt against payment (DAC-RAP) 84, 85
delivery risk 113
delivery versus payment (DVP) 84, 85, 134
delta hedge 26
derivative 3, 16
derivative products 2, 21, 116
Deutsche Aktien Index (DAX) 26, 27, 33, 38
Deutsche Bank 37
Deutsche Terminbörse (DTB) 22, 23, 26, 27, 28
Deutsche Wertpapierdaten-Zentrale GmbH (DWZ) 29
Deutscher Auslandskassenverein 134
Deutscher Kassenverein (DKV) 30, 141
DG bank 61
discount houses 14

dividend reinvestment plans 55, 56
dividend washing (France) 57
dividend (France) 55, 56, 57, 59, 61, 62, 64
dividend (Germany) 22, 29, 41
dividends 17, 109, 114, 118, 136, 137, 138, 141, 142, 143, 144, 146, 147
dividends (Japan) 78, 149
DKV, see Deutscher Kassenverein
domestic lending (Japan) 67, 72, 78, 79
Dresdner Bank 37
DRIP, see dividend reinvestment plans
Drysdale Government Securities Inc. 91, 92
Drysdale Securities Corporation 91, 103
DTB, see Deutsche Terminbörse
due-bill system (Japan) 67
DVP, see delivery versus payment
DVP settlement 134
DWZ, see Deutsche Wertpapierdaten-Zentrale GmbH

Echte Pensionsgeschäfte 143
Eligible Bank Bills 15
eligible bankers' acceptances 93
EOC, see Euroclear Operations Centre
equities 127
equivalent collateral 18
equivalent stock 18
ESM Government Securities Inc. 94
ESM Securities 91, 95
EUCLID 137, 139
Euroclear 31, 37, 102, 111, 117, 132, 133, 134, 135, 136, 138, 139
Euroclear Clearance System Société Cooperative 135
Euroclear Operations Centre (EOC) 135, 136, 137, 139
Euroclear Securities Lending and Borrowing Program 134, 136, 137
Euroclear Securities Settlement Processing 134, 135, 137
eurocommercial paper (ECP) 138
exchange risk 111

Federal Banking Supervisory Office (Bundesaufsichtsamt) 29
Federal Funds rate 86
Federal Open Market Committee (FOMC) 90
Federal Reserve 90, 93
Federal Reserve Act 90

Index

Federal Reserve Bank 92
finance type (Japan) 149
financial futures 21
Five Percent Rule of Large Holding (Japan) 77
flat pricing 91, 98
FOMC, see Federal Open Market Committee
forced deliveries 25
Foreign Exchange and Foreign Trade Control Act (Japan) 67, 73, 74
Frankfurter Kassenverein 30
French Bourse 47, 53
French Minibang 47
full-accrual pricing 92
Future structure of the Gilt Edged Market (Bank of England paper, 1985) 12
futures 6, 10, 13, 43, 64, 129
futures market (Germany) 22, 23, 27, 28

general collateral 96
General Electric 125
general stock loan operations (Japan) 66, 68, 71
German Civil Code, paragraph 607 41
German Commercial Code 143
German Custody Law 24
German gambling laws, paragraphs 762, 764 22, 23
German Income Tax Law 142
German Securities Data Centre 29
gilt market 17
gilts 13
gilt-edged market 16
gilt-edged securities 1, 9, 10, 15
global custody 116, 117, 118, 119, 120, 121, 122, 123
GNMA 87
Goldman Sachs 37
government bonds 5, 9
government bonds (Japan) 66
Government Securities Act 1986 95
Group of 30 (G30) 31, 53, 117
Group Suez 63

haircut 82, 91
Handelsblatt 28
hedge 2
hedge selling (Japan) 71
hedging futures (Germany) 22
hold-in-custody repo collateral 94, 95, 102

ICTA, 1988 18
identifiable bearer (France) 51
impot de bourse 148
income tax 18, 141, 142
income tax (Japan) 149
index options 16
Inland Revenue 10, 16, 18, 151
interest, accrued 98
interest rate risk 87
interest (Germany) 29
intermediaries 4, 5, 63, 132
Internal Revenue Code 152
international lending (Japan) 73, 75, 78, 79
inter-dealer brokers 10

J P Morgan 63
J P Morgan GmbH 20, 26, 37
Japan Securities Finance Co. Ltd 66, 67, 68, 69, 70, 71
Japanese Government Bonds 73
JASDAC 79
Joint Management Committee 12

Kassenverein Neu 25, 31
Kassenverein (KV) 24, 25, 27, 28, 29, 30, 31, 32, 33, 34, 36, 37, 38, 42, 45, 46
Kredietbank NV 127
Kreditbank SA Luxembourgeoise 127
KV, see Kassenverein
KV Neu, see Kassenverein Neu

Landesbanken 37
Landeszentralbank (LZB) 33
Letters of credit 5, 15, 110
letters of credit (Japan) 73, 76, 77
letters of guarantee (Japan) 76, 77
Libor 86, 99
LIFFE 16
LIFFE Bund contract 22, 26, 27
loan transactions (Japan) 68
Local Authority bonds 15
Lombard-Wall (LW) 91, 92, 93, 103
Lombard window 39
London Stock Exchange 10, 12, 15, 16, 17
LSB, see Landeszentralbank
LTOM 16
LW, see Lombard-Wall

Manual for Use of Assets 70

157

manufactured payments 151
marché des reports, see contango
margin 5
margin transactions (Japan) 66, 68
market crash 10
market maker 9, 10, 12, 13, 14, 15, 16, 18, 19, 49, 59, 137, 151
matched-sale-purchases (MSP) 90
MATIF 64
Merrill Lynch 37, 80, 82, 83, 98
minibang 50
minimum reserve regulations (Germany) 22, 39, 42, 43
Ministry of Finance (France) 61
Ministry of Finance (Japan) 78, 149
Mitsubishi Finance International 66
mochiai 69
MOF, see Ministry of Finance
money broker 13, 14, 15, 17, 18, 19, 151
money broking 9
monthly settlement market (France) 48, 59
Morgan Guaranty Trust Company of New York 135, 137, 138
Morgan Stanley 37, 116, 121
mortgage-backed pass-through securities 83
MSP, see matched-sale-purchases

NASD, see National Association of Securities Dealers
National Association of Securities Dealers (NASD) 95
net asset tax 141, 143
New Kassenverein 25
non-cash collateral (Japan) 77

Operation Liee 60
operational risk 108, 113, 114, 115
opportunity borrowers 137
opportunity lenders 31, 32, 137
options 6, 10, 13, 26, 27, 64, 65, 128
ordinary pension 60
Osaka Stock Exchange 50 Futures 72
ownership rights (Japan) 75

Paris Bourse 47, 59
pension livrée 61, 62, 65, 144
pension with delivery 47, 60, 61, 144, 145, 148
pensions (France) 60, 61, 148

Pensionsgeschäfte 143
policy investment stocks (Japan) 70
policy investment (Japan) 70, 71
political investment (Japan) 69, 70, 71
porteur identifiable, see identifiable bearer
preference shares 16
proxy voting 118
PSA, see Public Securities Association
Public Securities Association (PSA) 93
pure investment (Japan) 69, 70, 71
pure lending type (Japan) 149

ratios (France) 58
registration duties 148
Reglement Livraison Titres, see Relit
Relit 47, 51, 52, 53, 54, 55, 64
remere 47, 57, 59, 61, 62, 144, 146, 147, 148
repo (repurchase agreement) 37, 42, 43, 45, 47, 57, 59, 60, 64, 81, 82, 83, 84, 90, 91, 92, 93, 96, 98, 99, 101, 102, 103, 124, 141, 149, 150, 151, 152, 154
repo, collateral 83, 84, 85, 86, 88, 93, 94
repo, customer 90
repo, false 100, 101
repo, flex 84, 92
repo, hold-in-custody 85
repo, letter 85
repo, open 84, 93
repo, overnight 84, 86, 89
repo, reverse 39, 81, 82, 83, 86, 87, 88, 89, 90, 91, 92, 93, 94, 97
repo, system 90, 94
repo, term 84, 86, 89
repo, tri-party 85
repo, US Treasury 86
repo market 80, 82, 83, 90, 91, 95, 97, 101, 103
repo market (Germany) 39
repo money 86
repo rates 86, 87
repo transaction 83, 143, 153
repurchase agreement, see repo
repurchase transactions 143
Reserve Bank of New Zealand 134
reserve requirements (Germany) 23
reverse repo rates 87
reverse repurchase agreements 93
right to vote 18
rights 17, 41
rights issue 17
rights (France) 65
rights (Japan) 71

Index

risk weighting 10, 11
rolling settlement 19

Sale/Buyback 97, 98, 99
Salomon Brothers 37
Schelcher Prince 63
SEC 50, 103
Securities and Exchange Law (Japan) 66, 68
securities options 116
Securities Settlement Processing 136
securities transaction tax (Japan) 149, 150
sell and buyback (France) 60
SEPON 17
settlement 1, 2, 3, 4, 5, 12, 17, 18, 59, 80, 108, 116, 117, 119, 121, 124, 129, 132, 135, 136, 137
settlement bank 12, 13
settlement risk 113
settlement system (France) 52, 53, 54, 55, 64
settlement (Germany) 22, 24, 25, 29, 31, 34, 44, 45, 46
setlement (Japan) 76, 79
set-off 18
Shearson Lehman Brothers 37
short-term collateral certificates 17
Sicovam 49, 51, 52, 53, 55, 57, 58, 63, 64, 134
Simex Nikkei Average Futures 72
Société de Bourse 50
Société des Bourses Francaises 50
Société Générale 63
Société Interprofessionnelle pour la Conservation des Valeurs Mobilières, see Sicovam
Special Drawing Rights 139
stamp duty 4, 18, 146
stamp duty (France) 47, 60, 61
Standard and Poor's 94
standby letters of credit (Germany) 38
state central banks, see Landesbanken
Sterling Certificates of Deposit 15
Stock Exchange Turnover Tax 143

stock exchange turnover tax (Germany) 22, 23, 26
stock market crash 20, 24
subcustodian 118, 119, 121, 122
S.W.I.F.T. 125, 139

takeover 18
takeover offer 114
Talisman settlement system 17
TAURUS 16, 18, 19
Tokyo Stock Exchange 2, 67, 69
Topix 72
traded option market makers 16
traded options 2
transfer taxes 141, 143
Treasury and Eligible Bills 14
treasury bills 5
turnover tax 57, 59
Tuvier 50

UK Government Treasury Bills 15
Unechte Pensionsgeschäfte 143
Union Bank of Switzerland 127
US Bankruptcy court 93

Value Added Tax (VAT) Law 143, 146, 148, 149, 151
VAT (France) 58
vente à remere 59
voting right (Germany) 41
voting rights 109

warrants 127, 129, 134, 138
warrants (France) 50, 65
warrants (Japan) 71
withholding tax 150, 151
withholding tax (France) 55, 56, 57
withholding tax (Germany) 22, 23

zaibatsu 69, 70, 72

The following titles in the *Finance and Capital Markets* Series are also published by The Macmillan Press Ltd:

Bunds and Bund Futures   ISBN 0–333–56987–3

A practical guide to the German Government bond and futures markets, providing an overview of the market structure, its origins and developments and the role played by different participants. Discusses how bonds are issued, who trades and invests, the market system, the role of the Bundesbank, settlement and taxation.

November 1991   £75

Risk Management with Derivatives   ISBN 0–333–55924–X

The full implications of trading these products is examined in depth by leading practitioners in the field, focusing on the use of 3rd generation financial products such as swaps, futures and options, caps and swaptions.

September 1992   £75

Off Balance Sheet Finance   ISBN 0–333–56041–8

Written in the light of the Accounting Standards Board, this book discusses the various financing practices which have grown up over recent years and explains how they will be affected by the new accounting standard being developed by the ASB. It will provide an expert analysis of the accounting rules which will govern the treatment of off balance sheet finance when the standard comes into force.

December 1992   £95

For fuller information on these and other titles in the *Finance and Capital Markets* Series, or to order copies, please call on 0256 29242 or write to **Carla Jones, Globe Book Services Ltd, The Macmillan Press Ltd, Houndmills, Basingstoke, Hampshire RG21 2XS.**